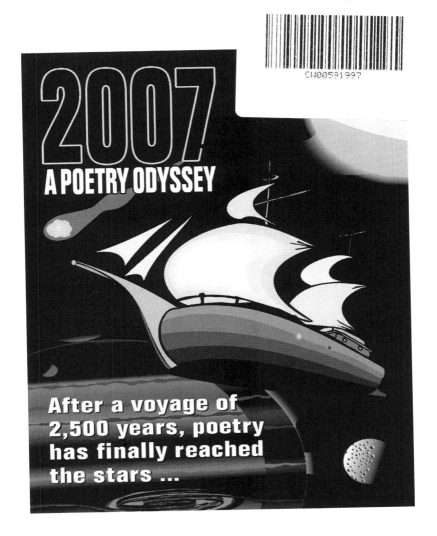

2007
A POETRY ODYSSEY

After a voyage of 2,500 years, poetry has finally reached the stars ...

East Midlands
Edited by Mark Richardson

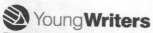
First published in Great Britain in 2007 by:
Young Writers
Remus House
Coltsfoot Drive
Peterborough
PE2 9JX
Telephone: 01733 890066
Website: www.youngwriters.co.uk

SB ISBN 978-1 84602 829 8

Foreword

This year, the Young Writers' *2007: A Poetry Odyssey* competition proudly presents a showcase of the best poetic talent selected from thousands of up-and-coming writers nationwide.

Young Writers was established in 1991 to promote the reading and writing of poetry within schools and to the young of today. Our books nurture and inspire confidence in the ability of young writers and provide a snapshot of poems written in schools and at home by budding poets of the future.

The thought, effort, imagination and hard work put into each poem impressed us all and the task of selecting poems was a difficult but nevertheless enjoyable experience.

We hope you are as pleased as we are with the final selection and that you and your family continue to be entertained with *2007: A Poetry Odyssey East Midlands* for many years to come.

Contents

Anthony Gell School, Wirksworth

Makhan Manraj Singh Johal (11)   109
Kelly Harland (11)   110
Ariel Draper (11)   111
Sharna Farrar (11)   112
James Pittham (11)   113
William Glasby (11)   114
Rafi Riaz (11)   115
Sarah Finan (12)   116
Georgia Watson (11)   117
Kurtis O'Sullivan (11)   118
Sophie Middleton (11)   119
Charli Blurton (11)   120
Alexandra Duesbury (11)   121
Alex Withey (12)   122
Bhavan Chahal (11)   123
Chris Brown (17)   124
Salma Moghal (17)   125
Chloe Tomlinson (18)   126
Alfie Wilson (17)   127
Heather Richardson (17)   128
Barnaby Lane (17)   129
Heidi Rudge (17)   130

Lees Brook Community Sports College, Derby

Jamie Woodside (11)   131
Lauren Decosta (11)   132
Heather Slater (11)   133
Laura Duxbury (11)   134
Maddison Ginn (12)   135
Taylor Stark (12)   136
Daniel Wilkinson   137
Lisa Miller (12)   138
Amy Cropley   139
Antonia Watts (12)   140
Samuel Kohrs (12)   141
Ryan Fitzhugh (12)   142
Callum Thompson (12)   143
Zavier Hobby (12)   144
Charlie Torry (13)   145
Christopher Swain (12)   146
Michael Toryusen (12)   147

Sir Jonathan North Community College, Leicester

The Poems

Every Day Is The Same

Every day is the same
people walking past me
as if nothing's there
worthless and invisible
that's me
an inch away from death
but thankful to survive.

Home wasn't much better
ignored and treated like vermin
an inch away from death
but thankful to survive.

Trying to be quiet in lessons
but screaming out inside
a friendless idiot
a waste of space
an inch away from death
but thankful to survive.

I'm a guitar
hollow and empty inside
unwanted - lost
an inch away from death
but thankful to survive.

But was I
yes, an inch away from death
but now
not thankful
but distraught
an inch away from death
but they should have left me to die.

Brogan Edwards (13)
Anthony Gell School, Wirksworth

Loneliness

Drained of all life inside you,
No one gives a care
Depressed, hollow and scared,
Still no one gives a care.

It was a depressing school day,
The sky was dark and grey
She suddenly began to ignore me,
The sky stayed dark and grey.

She started to begin to hear things,
The whistling of the wind
My friends began to hear things,
My voice, whistling in the wind.

A few days ago I was completely empty,
Depressed, hollow and scared
She came and explained all of what happened,
I was depressed, hollow and scared.

Drained of all life inside you,
But that was then, not now
Now I am full of life inside me,
We are friends, once again.

Charlotte Rapkin (13)
Anthony Gell School, Wirksworth

Lonely

I woke up
hollow and lonely
my mum is just a memory
slowly fading away.

School was awful
the friends weren't a help
all the sympathetic eyes
killing me inside.

I went to hockey club
it didn't take my mind off things
in fact it made it worse
oh God, just help me . . . please!

The day is ending
the sun's almost set
the pain is easing
but I know it's not over
- not quite yet.

Frances Kinder (13)
Anthony Gell School, Wirksworth

The Emptiest Time

It was the emptiest time in my life
I was left out in the cold,
No one really cared for me
When I was eight years old.

My life was just so useless
He beat me up all day,
Instead of lots of presents
I got hit on my birthday.

So my choice to run away from home
Seemed like the thing to do,
Instead I felt isolated
By people just like you.

I went back home to beg
But found he wasn't there,
So now my hole has been filled
My mum and me a pair.

Tim Richards (14)
Anthony Gell School, Wirksworth

Loneliness

I had a strange empty feeling inside,
I started to go cold,
My mind filled with freaky thoughts,
How could they? Why would they?

I sat on the bench,
I stared around the park,
There was no sign of them.
My stomach started to churn,
I had a massive lump in my throat,
A tear trickled down my cheek,
I felt so scared.
I looked at my phone,
It was dead,
I ran for my life,
I felt lonely.

Katie Dawes (13)
Anthony Gell School, Wirksworth

Loneliness

What are you running from?
You don't know yourself.
You're running from your loneliness,
you're running from your hell.

You feel broken inside,
tears roll down your face.
You are trying desperately,
to fill the empty space.

You walk down the alleyway,
and see me standing there,
come and stand beside me,
I won't stop and laugh I swear.

I understand your problems,
I understand your fear,
I'll listen to you closely
and I'll always be here.

I don't want you to be lonely,
so I will be your friend,
and if no one else will love you
I'll love you till the end.

Carrie Else (13)
Anthony Gell School, Wirksworth

A Dark Morning

A dark morning at the Taylors' house
It's as quiet as a mouse
Can I hear footsteps crawling down the stairs?
Is it a burglar hiding there?

The light turns on; I can now see it's not a burglar but my daddy
He gives me my brekkie
It's very yummy in my tummy.

Daddy leaves - I'm all alone
At the quiet Taylors' home.

Sad, sleepy and scared
I think of my daddy being out there.

Daddy's back! I run to the door
Now I feel safe and secure
See, being a dog is not such a bore!

Jack Taylor (13)
Anthony Gell School, Wirksworth

Darkness

The sun goes down, the night beckons,
It'll be up tomorrow or so it reckons,
Darkness penetrates the light once more,
It's done this silent fight before,
The battle goes on, only one can be victorious,
One of them will be the most glorious,
I know who will win, I've watched already,
I hug my knees and keep them steady,
The battle rages before my eyes,
The sun is filled with sorrowful sighs,
The sun gradually drifts down,
The darkness once more wears the crown,
I sit there mesmerised by the fight,
But soon enough it'll be light.

Seren Garner (11)
Anthony Gell School, Wirksworth

The Wonder Of Snowdonia

The jagged peaks,
the rolling hills,
all lying in the distance.
I watch,
I wait,
I see the wonder,
the wonder of Snowdonia.

The whistling wind,
the beating sun,
the weathers of the district.
I watch,
I wait,
I see the wonder,
the wonder of Snowdonia.

The mountain stands,
tall and proud,
lying in the distance.
I watch,
I wait,
I see the wonder,
the wonder of Snowdonia.

I must now leave,
leave behind the beauty,
I look behind,
the wonder of Snowdonia.

Sarah Allsop (12)
Anthony Gell School, Wirksworth

Wish

I wish for happiness for everyone.
And that all mean thoughts will be gone.

I wish that we wouldn't pass on.
Not just family and friends, everyone.

I wish for laughter to fill the streets.
To pass on our happiness to everyone we meet.

I wish for all wars to end.
So everyone could just be friends.

This would be great; but don't you see,
That this can't happen; this can't be.

Because we can't live if we can't die.
We can't laugh if we can't cry.
There's no truth if we can't lie.
We can't love if we can't hate.
We can't sleep if we can't wake.
There's no happy if there's no sad.
There's no good if there's no bad.
There's no peace if there's no war.
There's no other way. There's no more.
That's it. It's just a law.

Daisy Hopley (11)
Anthony Gell School, Wirksworth

Loneliness

In the corner
She hides from her.
In the corner
She hides from Sir.

In the corner
She has no one to love.
In the corner
She has a pet bird - a dove.

In the corner
Her back turned away.
In the corner
She has nothing to say.

In the corner
Her life goes slowly.
In the corner
She calls herself lonely.

Sarah Chamberlain (13)
Anthony Gell School, Wirksworth

The Loneliness Of Homelessness

How would you feel if it were you,
Sleeping rough, brought down with flu,
The cold winter nights that never end,
The constant loneliness, driving you round the bend?

How would you feel if you were there too,
If you slept rough and had the flu,
Think of the cold winter nights,
All the things you want to do, but all the mights?

What if it were you,
And you had no friends to comfort you,
You are all alone so what can you do,
Call for help, but to who?

Who will help you when you're on the street,
Who will give to you when you plead?
You will have no one to go and meet,
Money is something that you need.

Though they don't understand why you plead,
Why you left home with such a need,
They don't see why you have no friends,
They just keep walking, and walking round that bend.

Matthew Daldorph (13)
Anthony Gell School, Wirksworth

I'm Wearing Thin

I'm wearing thin
Wearing out, becoming weak
Holding hands with this rogue, it's myself,
Destructive. Yet now I see it's you that's tearing me,
Ensnaring me, this is my dying in your arms,
I cut you out so, set me free.
But I can't make it on my own,
Because my heart won't live alone
So cut my wrists and black my eyes.
So I can fall asleep tonight, or die,
Because you kill me. You poisoned my life.
So I take this knife, and I cut you out.

I'm on my own, the loneliness finally hitting my heart . . .
Hitting my home.

Katie Taylor (13)
Anthony Gell School, Wirksworth

Days

Monday
Monday morning here again
got to catch the bus
got to go and meet my friend
now I have to rush.

Tuesday
Tuesday comes around so fast
the alarm goes off again
I was in such a deep, deep sleep
it sounded like Big Ben.

Wednesday
Wednesday is here, it's the middle of the week
my first lesson is maths
school work is so boring
I'd rather be at the baths.

Thursday
Thursday came and went so fast
now I'm on the bus
got to hurry into class 'cause I don't want to be the last
now I've really got to rush.

Friday
Friday has come last but not least
I am off the bus
ready for a midnight feast
now I've not got to rush off the bus.

Levis Barber (11)
Anthony Gell School, Wirksworth

Spring, Summer, Autumn, Winter

Spring is the time when the flowers start to grow.
Colours start to appear and still grow and grow.
Summer is the time when everything is fine.
Flowers are here and now have appeared.
Autumn is where the flowers have died.
They go all brown and fall to the ground.
Winter is cold and the flowers are dead,
But never mind, they will be back again.

Jade Birks (12)
Anthony Gell School, Wirksworth

Sailing

I like sailing it's real fun,
Sometimes it gets nasty and very soggy!
But it's always best in the sun.
My dad works 5 days a week,
To earn the cash,
To buy my cool yacht called Panache!
I've sailed her only once,
And my mum fell in!
When she got out she smelt like a year-old dustbin!
I saw Ellen MacArthur on a fun day at Carsington Water,
She even had her own chauffeur to escort her!
Every night I dream on,
That I will become like Ellen MacArthur,
And be the one.

Lucy Miller (11)
Anthony Gell School, Wirksworth

The Big Game

The whistle has gone,
the game has begun.
Two teams they are,
one winner there is.

Passing to players,
tackling their team,
scoring goals, we are.

Second half now,
the players refreshed.
Scoring more goals,
that's the end of it now.

Passing to players,
tackling their team,
scoring goals, we are.

Alex Hopkinson (11)
Anthony Gell School, Wirksworth

Arsenal

Arsenal, Arsenal, Arsenal,
What would we do without them?
Arsenal, Arsenal, Arsenal,
When we score we hear them roar,
Arsenal, Arsenal, Arsenal,
When we win we shout for him,
Arsenal, Arsenal, Arsenal,
Wonder goal! Wonder goal! Wonder goal!
What would we do without him?
Scoring and battling,
Arsenal, Arsenal, Arsenal,
We play our rivals, Spurs,
Arsenal, Arsenal, Arsenal,
Henry scores this third,
Arsenal, Arsenal, Arsenal,
A win in the bag and Spurs are sad,
Ha ha ha!

Ryan Marchington (11)
Anthony Gell School, Wirksworth

The Autumn Magpie

A flash of black,
A streak of white,
A flutter of wings -
Now he's in flight,
For he's the autumn magpie.

He never pinches,
He never steals,
He only borrows,
For he's the autumn magpie.

Fast as a bullet,
As swift as an arrow,
For he's the autumn magpie.

If it's shiny it's gone,
Keys, rings and watches too,
For he's the autumn magpie.

Winter is coming,
He's taken his turn
And now he has to go.

A flash of black,
A streak of white,
A flutter of wings -
Now he's in flight.
For he's the autumn magpie.
Yes - he's the autumn magpie.

Eliza Day (11)
Anthony Gell School, Wirksworth

The Storm

The sky alight like fire,
Forks of lightning throttling the sky,
Blackness, darkness, becoming lightness,
The peacefulness slowly beginning to die.

Rumbling, rumbling, rumbling, bang!
Thor at his best, making the sky come alive,
The noise like a bear's stomach when he's hungry,
The lightning going everywhere, darting and diving.

The rain pounding down like stones,
Falling from the sky,
Pounding the puddles when they fall,
Like gunshots coming from the skies.

Rain falling from the sky like blue sweets
Falling into a puddle's mouth,
Rippling every time they fall then the ripples slip away
Like they were never there.

Water, water, water,
Everywhere, flooding the land,
Flowing, rushing, speeding,
The river rising up, up, up.

Trees blowing like a giant blowing his nose,
The noise like nothing no one's ever heard,
Crashing, banging . . . the storm.

Then the noise dies down gradually,
The sun comes out and the storm is no more.

Evie Allsop (11)
Anthony Gell School, Wirksworth

Funny Poem

I was born in Nottingham City Hospital in 1995.
I dived out of my mummy's tummy,
The midwife shouted, 'He's alive!'
My aunt said, 'Here, have some money.'
Away we went in the car home,
We accidentally hit a gnome,
Before we knew six years had passed,
We never thought it would last,
Off I ran up to school,
I always had to sit on a stool,
Later on I turned ten,
My dad bought me a pet hen,
Here I am now, age eleven,
Living not that far from the River Severn.

Joshua Robinson (11)
Anthony Gell School, Wirksworth

The View From My Window

Cows grazing in the field,
The trees swaying in the wind,
A dog in the farmyard,
The clouds move lazily across the sky,
Cooking apples ready to fall to the ground,
Rabbits bouncing across the field,
The weathervane on the barn points to the south,
This is the view from my window.

Riah Maskrey (11)
Anthony Gell School, Wirksworth

Dreams, Dreams, Dreams

Dreams, dreams, dreams,
Oh how I wish . . .
The silent whinny of my horse,
The sound of hooves, *clip-clip, clip-clop,*
The swish of the tail,
The crunching, munching on the hay,
Oh how I wish some way, some day.
Maybe a walk or maybe a canter,
Maybe a jump or maybe a wander,
Dreams, dreams, dreams,
Oh how I wish.

Amy Maycock (11)
Anthony Gell School, Wirksworth

A 'Break' In The Sun

At age 7 I broke my arm
Mum found it hard to keep me calm.
I felt upset, it made me cry
A week later to Corfu we were to fly.

I left A&E with my arm in a pot
The Mediterranean would I see, maybe not.
My friends wanted to sign my cast
Mum said 'no', so it would last.

I was able to enjoy my holiday
My broken arm did not get in the way.
I wore a bag to keep it dry
I could swim and do sports, the time flew by.

When we got back home off it came
My arm had healed and felt the same.
When we're about to have a break in the sun
My mum warns me to be careful while having fun.

Ellie Tomlinson (12)
Anthony Gell School, Wirksworth

Mystery Mare

Nose as soft as velvet,
Coat as smooth as silk,
Tail long and flowing,
Blaze as white as milk.

Galloping across the sunset,
Clearing the jump but not by too much,
Soaring like an angel,
Responding to every touch.

Her favourite treats are carrots,
She loves to roll in mud,
Food, she tells me, is her favourite thing,
She talks to me you know.

She loves, I think (apart from food)
A gelding named Brad,
He once tried to kiss her bum,
But to him she was quite bad.

Her body gives off a lovely heat,
I love to snuggle her close,
Her ears prick, she knows I'm there,
I love her the most.

So have you guessed yet who she is?
It is of course,
Hannah, our beautiful bay horse.

Jade Boam (11)
Anthony Gell School, Wirksworth

The Fairground

Rides are rocking
The clock is tocking
As the ride is moving
The music is grooving

As I approach the sugary stand
I get my money out of my pocket with my hand
Hot dogs, chips and ginger beer
Are now about to reappear

At the fun house
I see a tiny mouse
The lights are flashing
The bumper cars are bashing

The queue for the waltzers is very long
I start to hum along to the song
As we are spinning around and around
I look to the floor to see what I have found

As everybody decides to go home
I have to walk home all on my own
As I walk through the door
I can remember all the things that I saw.

The fairground.

Rianne Wetton (11)
Anthony Gell School, Wirksworth

Football/Friends

F riends are made through football,
O ne or two or three.
O nce we're all together
T here's just no stopping me.
B oot it up the field,
A ll the way up.
L et's try and score a goal,
L et's try and win the cup!

D ancing round defenders,
E ating up midfield,
R unning rings around goalies,
'B oot it,' someone squealed
Y es! it's a goal.

C ome on, you can win,
O nce you've got your friends,
U nderstanding,
N ow you've won,
T hat teams are made through friends
Y ou can always rely upon.

Aaron Taylor (11)
Anthony Gell School, Wirksworth

Pony Maniac

I'm just a pony maniac
Cos ponies are contagious,
If I'm not around them
I might become dangerous,
If you don't like them
Then you must be ridiculous.
Ponies are wickedly marvellous
When I ride 'em they just become fast and furious.
When a pony is my favourite I'm very generous,
When they are around me I'm oblivious,
So I'm just a pony maniac,
It's obvious.

Olivia Tallis (11)
Anthony Gell School, Wirksworth

The Autumn Sun

The autumn sun shone through the trees,
Leaves of shades of brown, falling in the breeze.
The sight of squirrels gathering winter food,
Always makes me in the autumn mood.

So many colours not just green and brown,
I am so grateful to see what's around.
The smells and sounds of nature's gift,
As I walk along they slowly drift.

As the wispy leaves brush against my feet,
A field mouse scurries away.
The graceful wind in my hair
I can see the animals doing their share.

Emma Harris (11)
Anthony Gell School, Wirksworth

The Sea Is A Magical Place

The sea is a magical place,
grasping a thousand secrets,
nobody knows what's really there,
beneath the myths and the stories.

Many sailors cross its depths,
struggling to survive,
you may have found that few of them,
manage to return alive.

Its graceful waves and elegance,
tend to fool most,
the sea is very powerful,
the sea is a magical place.

Connie Hobbs (12)
Anthony Gell School, Wirksworth

Grandma

I look at her and see
What I will see
In 69 years' time
Like a mirror.

The mirror shatters
Like her mind
As brittle as bones
Who are you?

Photos of strangers, but
People she knew
Visits from friends
Who fill in the hours.

Steady rhythm of
Life passing by
Ready meals and
Bleepers for wardens.

Stuck in her past
Full of crumbling history
Reminders of Lincoln
Am I there?

I look at her hands
See all the lines carved in
Like roads where
She's been in her life.

Eyes innocently blink
That once looked
At the reflection of her youth
72 years ago.

Her hands reach out
For balance
Something to hold.
Something to love.

My grandma.

Elizabeth Hobbs (18)
Anthony Gell School, Wirksworth

Autumn

Leaves are falling,
nights are drawing in,
feeling the need for a blanket
as there's an extra chill in the air.

Mists hang low in valleys,
grey and ghostly,
reminding me that the season
of bonfires and Hallowe'en is near.

Trees and bushes full of fruit,
people start to make their pies.

Eating in front of roaring fires
with the curtains tightly shut.

Elizabeth Whittall (11)
Anthony Gell School, Wirksworth

Birds

Birds are quick
Birds are fast.
They fly around
With a laugh.
Their laugh is happy
Their laugh is sweet.
They sing
With a tweet.

Tina Hulley (11)
Anthony Gell School, Wirksworth

Food

My favourite meal of the day
probably pasta I would say
its heavenly taste
with a sprinkle of cheese
make it taste as sweet as honey made by the bees
I also like it filled with ham
which makes my mouth water
with a bit of pepper that makes you sneeze
which makes it so perfect
I like a glass of strawberry milkshake
and for my pudding I would like
some fresh lemon drizzle cake
fresh out the oven.

Edward Boam (11)
Anthony Gell School, Wirksworth

Bobby And Henry

On the third of November,
As the days were turning cold,
Two puppies were born;
One black, one gold.

The week before Christmas,
We gave them a home,
We gave them names
And they started to roam.

Blackie and Goldie
Were their temporary names,
They explored the outside,
Down the snow-covered lanes.

By the hot crackling fire,
They lay warm and snug,
Life was so easy,
And the world a big rug.

Puppies no longer,
They should be mature,
But they bounce and they bark
As I walk through the door.

Bobby and Henry
Both family and friends,
Such faithful companions,
Their love never ends.

Emily Bathie (11)
Anthony Gell School, Wirksworth

Summertime

Summertime is full of fun,
Enjoying yourself, lapping up the sun.
The only way of keeping cool
Is splashing around in an ice-cold pool.
Sitting on a deckchair grabbing a tan,
Having a sip from a refreshing can.
Watching the bees swarming about,
Whilst the birds are tweeting in the clouds.
Cooking some food on the barbecue,
Waiting for friends that are overdue.
That is what my favourite time of year is all about,
Vivid blue skies, not a single cloud.
But sadly winter is nearly here,
Never mind, there's always next year.

Lauren Garratt (12)
Anthony Gell School, Wirksworth

All Things Random And Odd

If you were a duck, then you would be in luck.
'You see,' said he, to a tree and a bee,
'Being a bag would suck.'

Now the bee who was actually a bag,
Pondered this thought at tea.
If being a bag is as bad as a hag,
Then I'm better off as a pea.

Somewhere on the planet of beer,
(Which was famous for giving a cheer),
Someone found out, and gave a big shout.
'The land of normal is near!'

Daisy Howstan (11)
Anthony Gell School, Wirksworth

Snow

The snow had fallen through the night,
Very soft and very white,
It covered the grass,
It covered the trees,
Swishing and swirling in the breeze.

The sky turned red,
The sun arose,
But down in the valleys,
Trees still froze.

Up in the park,
Out on the ice,
Children skating, and sliding,
Don't they look nice!

Down in the town;
Where the sun can't see,
There are icicles hanging everywhere,
Waiting to drop and stab me.

Cinder eyes and old top hat,
On the garden bench is where he's sat,
Tomorrow just a heap of snow,
Oh dear me, where did our snowman go?

Daniel Hopkinson (11)
Anthony Gell School, Wirksworth

The Unseen Predator

Lurking in the murky water,
Amongst the stems of weeds,
An unseen predator lies waiting,
For the thing on which it feeds.

Its powerful jaw,
Full of razor-sharp teeth,
Shows no mercy,
To the prey it may eat.

Patiently waiting,
A fish comes into sight,
The powerful creature attacks,
The winner is the pike.

Daniel Drewry (11)
Anthony Gell School, Wirksworth

Hunting, Shooting, Fishing

The bang of the gun as it sights its brace.
The swish of the rod with its fly poised to become a meal.
The bark of the hounds as they pursue their prey.
The splash of the streamlined fish when it comes jumping
                                    and leaping out of the water.
The thud of the beautiful pheasant when it falls out
                                    of the large majestic oak.
The sound of the bugle loud and proud over the many acres
                                    of forest and lush green fields.
These are the traditions of the countryside.

Miles Curtis (11)
Anthony Gell School, Wirksworth

Love

Love is a river, a river that gently flows with no connections broken.
Love is a gift that should be handled carefully.
Love is our past, our present and our future.
Love is a rainbow, you never know when it ends.
Love is sharing, forgiveness and kindness.
Love is flowers blooming up all over the world.
Love is a plane, you never know where you might end up.
Love is a friendship that lasts to eternity.
Love is a special bond between two people.
Love is fruit, fresh and ripe.
Love is strong, beautiful and great.
Love makes you feel warm inside.
Love makes you feel really special.
Love can be anything, but really it all comes down to one thing,
Love is a promise, a secret that should be kept forever!

Alana Barrett (12)
Anthony Gell School, Wirksworth

My Two Guinea Pigs

They are cute and cuddly,
One is called Jumpy,
He can be very grumpy,
Jumpy runs at great speeds,
With his eyes popping out like beads.

The other one is called Nibbles,
He is so white and fluffy,
And sometimes he gets so scruffy,
He eats lots of food
Which puts him in a good mood.

They make such a squeak,
When they get treats,
They both love each other,
Because they are such lovely brothers.

Sonya Betts (12)
Anthony Gell School, Wirksworth

Football

Football is wicked
Football is great
It's the best game
That I have ever played.

Take on a player
Make the ball roll
Take on the keeper
Score a great goal.

Your team is winning
It's near the end
The whistle's gone
You have won again.

Ryan Smith (11)
Anthony Gell School, Wirksworth

The Angry Sea . . . The Calm Sea

This is the sea that everyone likes,
The one that does as it's told . . .

Gently washing away the sand,
Flowing from side to side,
As I walk along it hugs my feet,
Whilst tickling me between my toes,
As it dances around it will stroke the rocks,
And leap around with joy,
As it draws to night it would settle down,
Into a deep relaxing sleep.

But this sea is different,
Very different . . .

Smashing and crashing while storming around,
Nothing could stop it now,
For this sea there are no boundaries,
It will go as far as it can,
Hitting the rocks as it goes on by,
You wouldn't want to get in the way.
Then it comes to night and it just gets worse,
Keeping everyone else awake.

Rosie Dixey (11)
Anthony Gell School, Wirksworth

My Cat

My cat was called Willow
He loved to sleep on a pillow
He had a toy mouse
That he loved to bring in the house

He sat on my knee
While I watched TV
When I stroked his nice warm fur
He would just purr, purr, purr.

He was a little bit blind
But never mind
He bumped into this
And he bumped into that.

He died one Christmas time
That precious cat was all mine
Goodbye Willow
Sleep tight on your pillow.

Sian Taylor (11)
Anthony Gell School, Wirksworth

A Man's Best Friend

When you're down and troubled and you need some loving care
I would like to tell you who could be there,
A man's best friend is a friend for life,
You could try one instead of a wife.
He will be there for you always, when you need him the most.
When you look into his eyes, you think to yourself,
He is the one for me.
You're never alone with him by your side,
And he'll fill your heart with love and pride.

James Day (11)
Anthony Gell School, Wirksworth

Music

It's a beat,
It's a rhythm,
It's a song without words,
It's rock,
It's soul,
It's a tune from the birds.

It brings the world together,
It can bring peace,
When there's music in the air,
You breathe it
And give it,
It's something you share.

There is so much,
It can soar,
It can fly,
But I'll never hear it all
If I search,
Or if I try.

Becky Scott (11)
Anthony Gell School, Wirksworth

Homeless

Do you know what it feels like to be homeless
and have nobody to love you?
I sit in a shelter
watching the world go by
every now and again I get a smile from someone,
it feels great, maybe they like me!
My stomach rumbles every night as people walk past
with chips and nice warm drinks.
What do I get? Nothing, every now and again
I get a drink and chocolate bar but what's that?
My feet go numb and I can't get to sleep!
It snows and as it falls to the ground
I get a shiver down my spine.
Soon be summer, maybe I might get some sleep.

Maybe someone in the world might love me! But who?

Lucy Maycock (13)
Anthony Gell School, Wirksworth

Nothing I'm Doing . . .

Sitting here all alone,
Nothing I'm doing but freezing to the bone.
So how did I end up on the street?
Nothing I'm doing but freezing my feet.
People see me and think, *how did he end up like that?*
Nothing I'm doing but trying to tap.
So sitting here feeling that life is bleak,
Nothing I'm doing but thinking, *is this my peak?*
So life is pointless, now what should I do?
Nothing I'm doing but talking to you.
So here I am, feeling low,
Nothing I'm doing and nowhere to go.
So tell me what to do now I'm confused,
Nothing I'm doing and I'm not amused.
So tell me now, is this the end?
Nothing I'm doing but asking, 'Any change to lend?'
So here I am feeling blue,
Nothing I'm doing but discussing you.
So here I'm saying goodbye my friend,
Nothing I'm doing but narrating my end!

Philip Whitehead (13)
Anthony Gell School, Wirksworth

The Lonely Boy

The lonely boy who travels all alone,
The lonely boy who has no home,
The lonely boy who has no one to care,
The lonely boy who has nothing to spare,
The lonely boy was oh so sad,
The lonely boy had no dad,
The lonely boy was only a child,
The lonely boy had to live in the wild,
The lonely boy was always cold,
The lonely boy has no one to hold,
The lonely boy lives on the street,
The lonely boy gets cold feet,
The lonely boy had friends, *if* only,
The lonely was very, very lonely.

Nichol Scott (13)
Anthony Gell School, Wirksworth

Homeless

Find a doorstep with no one around,
the cold hits your spine -
as you sit on the ground.
You toss and turn all night long,
and you get a whiff of that stale pong.
Rubbish scattered all around,
but you can't hear anything, not a sound.
A torch like a star shines in your eyes,
you pick up your pack and walk into the night.
Strolling the streets all day long,
asking for change - to buy some food,
everyone stares like you don't belong,
so you walk away -
hoping tomorrow is a better day!

Sophie Redgrave (13)
Anthony Gell School, Wirksworth

I'm Lonely

I'm lonely and I'm waiting for a friend to come and join me . . .
I'm lonely and I'm waiting for people to love me,
To care for me and to be there for me when I'm down . . .
I'm lonely and I can taste the salt from my tears
That run into my mouth . . .
I'm lonely and my life is a big disaster, my parents don't care,
I don't want to take part in this world anymore . . .
I'm lonely and I don't get a wink of sleep at night,
I don't speak to anybody, I daren't, I don't know what to say,
Nobody ever talks to me . . .
I'm lonely and I'm sick of all the arguing, name calling,
Bullying and discomfort from all the pupils . . .
I'm sick of all of this! I'm lonely, lonely, lonely!
You only have one life and I feel on the outside of mine!
Why are they ruining my life? Why me? Why?

Laura Marchington (13)
Anthony Gell School, Wirksworth

Alienated

Empty, disliked, hurt,
They're always talking about me.
'The pit', invisible, unwanted,
I feel like a homeless child.
Ashamed, stone-cold, friendless,
The sky is dark and grey.
Will they always stop talking when I come over?
Will I always feel lonely and bored?

Hollow, abandoned, deserted,
This is what I always feel like.
Drained, unwanted, grieving,
It's like I'm always wrong.
Insecure, lost, left out,
I'm worthless as a penny.
Will I always be unimportant?
Will I always be a useless girl?

Stupid, blank, cold,
My group of friends have left me.
I don't know why this is happening,
However, it's what it's like to be friendless.
Will I feel like this forever?
Will I live the same old distraught, ruined life?
Who knows? Not me, not you - no one!

Sara Shortland (13)
Anthony Gell School, Wirksworth

The Man And His Cat

There was a man who kept cats,
Their purpose was catching the rats,
The man became hazy
And his cats became lazy,
So now they're driving him bats!

Laura Robinson (11)
Belper School, Belper

Eldar Call Of War

People hide,
Armies gather,
Plans are made,
That's the Eldar call of war.

Guns bang,
People scream,
Fire burns,
That's the Eldar call of war.

Blood runs,
Anger rises,
Death wakes,
That's the Eldar call of war.

Elliot Heeley (11)
Belper School, Belper

Sweets

Sweets, bonbons, chocolates or éclairs,
These are the things that make me tear our my hair!
My eyes go pop and my cheeks go spotty!
My lips suck inwards! I have to sit on a potty!
So never give me sweets, bonbons, chocolates or éclairs
'Cause these are the things that make me tear out my hair!

Catherine Johnston (11)
Belper School, Belper

My Horrible Aunt

My auntie Jan
She was actually a man
She liked to use her frying pan
But not to cook some food within
It was to cook my guinea pig Jim.

She cooked and cooked and cooked and cooked
As so, horrified, I looked
Jan turned around and said, 'Don't worry,
I'm going to put him in a curry.'

The smell I smelt was so horrific
But my aunt just said, 'Terrific!'
I cried and cried and cried and cried
But my aunt just lied and lied.

'I did not cook that horrible beast
You did, you had it for a feast.'
'You nasty aunt, you must be a man
You cooked my pet in a frying pan!'

Joanne Brewer (11)
Belper School, Belper

Five Tall Oak Trees

Five tall oak trees
Standing on the floor,
Lightning struck the first one
Then there were four.

Four tall oak trees
Homes for a bee,
The family needed paper
Then there were three.

Three tall oak trees
Making firewood for you,
Men came and chopped it down
Then there were two.

Two tall oak trees
All their friends had gone,
A man wanted furniture
Then there was one.

One tall oak tree
Standing all alone,
Children playing with fire
Then there were none.

Abigail Noble (11)
Belper School, Belper

The Last Teacher

The last teacher we had was Mrs Cran,
Assigned to our class on Monday.
It's only because Mr Luzz left the school last Sunday.
The teacher before that was Mrs Pratt, and boy was she a pain.
But after three days of teaching us no one saw her again.
I think before that we had a man, his name was Mr Snare.
He only left because we put superglue on his chair.
But let's go back to the start and I'll talk about Mrs Cran.
Her nightmare lasted about a week, and this was how it began . . .

It's day number one; she's here with Miss Rime,
Our tricks are ready; she's right on time.

It's day number two; she's a real old nag,
But we've put a stink bomb in her bag.

It's day number three; she's still here,
So we swapped her water for mouldy beer!

It's day number four; why won't she leave?
But in her car there's a hive of bees.

It's day number five; we can't give in.
So we've put her trainers in the bin.

It's day number six; time for plan H,
In her drawer there's a rubber snake.

It's day number seven; she's not gone,
We're starting to feel that she's won.
Her lessons are *pants*, but we'll give her a chance . . .
Maybe she's the one.

I'm the new teacher, Mrs Cran, assigned to their class forever.
They tried their best but I won't rest and now we're a class together.

Ellie Hutton (13)
Belper School, Belper

Dark Nights

One dark night I crept into a big scary house,
With creaky floorboards, or was it a squeak of a big fat mouse!

I wondered what I was going to find,
As I climbed the spiral staircase,
It was dark and eerie,
The chilled breeze blew the curtains made from lace.

A shiver went down my spine,
As a ghost popped out from nowhere,
Argh! I ran for my life,
Was this real or just a terrible nightmare?

Down the spiral staircase,
Across the creaky floor and out the door,
To a bright sunny day,
I woke from that place that was now no more.

Victoria Trow (12)
Belper School, Belper

Moths

They flitter and fly around the night sky
Attracted to lights, sweets and wine
You will find them almost anywhere
They are the real fairies at the bottom of your garden.

Moths come big, small, microscopic and massive
You get the eggars and the emperors
And the hawks with the underwings
Can you count how many species there are?

Their caterpillars are amazing
They can look like elephant trunks or even part of a flower
Demolishing leaves and troughing through fuchsias
Caterpillars are hairy, funny coloured and unstoppable!

Camouflaged excellently
Some moths are hidden from the inexperienced eye
A few resemble broken-off twigs
And others look like small mammals.

They range in size from macro to micro
Some whoppers with a wingspan over five inches
While others have less than half an inch
But most of them fall into the size in-between.

Moths come in a lot of different colours
And these are only a few:
They are red and yellow and green and brown
And black and chocolate and mauve and cream
And crimson and silver and grey and purple
And white and pink and orange and blue.

So if you are about on a summer's eve
Watch out! Watch out! There are moths about!

Sam Milward (12)
Belper School, Belper

School Dinners

Some are horrid, some are nice,
Macaroni cheese, vanilla ice.
Some can be healthy, some not,
Apple crumble, beef hotpot.
Some may be tasty, some may be nasty,
Chips and beans with Cornish pasty.
Dinner ladies stand, in their caps,
Treacle sponge and ginger snaps.
Here I wait with a rumbling tum,
Yorkshire pudding or maybe a plum?
We get to the corner, what's for lunch?
Shepherd's pie and chocolate crunch!

Charlotte England (12)
Belper School, Belper

My Ideal World

My ideal world is equal.
My ideal world is fair.
There's no poverty, no hunger
And no polluted air.

Countryside surrounds us.
Polar bears have ice.
War is a thing of the past
And there's no extinct wildlife.

The real world is changing -
Changing all the time.
If we come together,
Our world could be like mine!

Sadie Maher (11)
Belper School, Belper

The Sound Of Life Passing Me By

As life is passing me by,
I hear the wind rushing.
The cows crying out make me think of a farm.
Hearing the birds calling is like a daughter calling to its mother.

Motorbikes zooming down the street,
Like a bee in a bottle.
The sound of an aeroplane makes me want to fly,
As life is passing me by.
I don't know why.
I sit and think about this as a train goes by.

All of the cars have a type of sound.
The sound of cars chuntering by at 4am.

No one seems to understand the journey of a car.
The car ignition turns . . .
Just as the wind makes the leaves rustle.

The mobile phone rings . . . no one answers.
The caller is the sound of life passing me by.
Life passing me by!

All of the objects were made by sound.

Sarah Moore (11)
Belper School, Belper

Noises

At the front of my house
The noises are
The twittering of a dickie bird
The vroom of a car.

The music from the bandstand
The rustling of the leaves
The miaowing of the little cat
The little cat called Peeves.

The engine of the train
Louder than a mouse
These are the noises
From the front of my house.

Laura Marriott (11)
Belper School, Belper

Tiger

Forest walker
Land stalker
Man scratcher
Prey catcher
Night prowler
Heavy growler
Food seeker
Never weaker.

Adie Lee (11)
Belper School, Belper

Deep Down Under The Sea

Deep down under the sea,
There's a monster waiting for me,
He was my friend he told me,
But, now I believe it was just a story,
He was a merman, a king of mermen he claimed,
And foolishly I asked, I asked him to explain,
He told me of peril and danger,
I should never have spoken to this terrible stranger,
For now I know his true history,
The rest was just a made up story,
Deep down under the sea,
There's a monster waiting for me.

Joanna Saunders (11)
Belper School, Belper

Jim The Cat

Jim was a cat with only one ear,
He was black and sleek and shiny
And revelled in hate and fear.
His eyes were amber, his teeth were sharp,
His favourite food was the fishy carp.

Jim had a best friend, Kevin by name,
Kevin liked to play, Kevin liked a game.
One day Kevin gave Jim a playful leer,
It was in that fatal play fight, that Jim lost his ear.

Jim was a cat with a reputation to keep,
He liked to pounce on rivals and hiss at nearby sheep.
Jim was very warlike, like an ancient Gaul in fact,
And attracted female felines using loads of skill and tact.

First, very softly, he'd make a noise like a bee,
Then he'd purr cutely for all females to see,
Then he'd call to Kevin, his furry feline friend,
Then they'd have a fight, or so they'd both pretend.

Jim was leader of the neighbourhood cats,
Kevin was just below, in vice president stats,
Jim ruled the troublemakers with an iron fist,
A record of the fights he'd had would be a never-ending list.

Jim discovered an enemy with a rather nasty bark,
And just to prove who was boss Jim attacked him in the dark,
The dog wasn't evil so he and Jim became chums,
They often spent their evenings with Kevin in the slums.

Jim liked lamp posts,
Liked to bash them with his head,
He rammed one too hard one day,
It's a shame 'cause now he's dead.

James Stephenson (11)
Belper School, Belper

Think

Today I was called a name
'Fatty', 'Piggy', they're all the same
I look in the mirror and I think
Think about the people
Think about the pain
More and more the tears trickle down my cheeks
They pierce my skin with darkness
I undress and look
I see the greed that caused this pain
I see the cuts on my wrists, more pain.
I think I'm doomed to a life of misery
And I know I'm right.
People say I'm beautiful
People say they care.
But nobody cares, I have nobody
I think.

Poppy Grey (13)
Belper School, Belper

My Brother

Meet my brother,
An extreme animal lover!
Here are a few of his pets; he has . . .
5 rabbits, 7 guinea pigs
5 dogs, 3 cats
6 budgies, 2 parrots
15 fish, 4 horses
3 donkeys, 2 snakes
5 spiders, 3 rats
4 tortoises, 7 lizards
11 mice and 5 hamsters!
If this isn't enough I also have 4 brothers
And 5 sisters and 3 cousins!
So as you are thinking in your head right now,
You can put up with this how?
Well it's hard you see,
But leave a space in your heart for poor little me!

Rachel Mason (11)
Belper School, Belper

Windy Whirl

An innocent daisy,
the last one of spring.
Oh no, the wind is going to sing,
he will blow off my petals,
end my life, make me go
and lose my flow.
One petal down, five to go,
as I cry, no, no, no.
Gripping tight in the light,
and all through the long hot night.
In the morn, the rise of the sun,
two petals left, no friends in sight,
please, please, please,
stop this fright!
You have had your chance,
it's over for you and this is what I'm going to do.
After a blow it started to snow
and a whole two seasons had passed.
It would never last.
Flowers must go, heave and ho,
to leave us with white, deep snow.
Now who did this terrible thing?
Who didn't let them sing?
Who finished this love twirl?
Oh yeah, it must be the Windy Whirl!

Carly Alice Tomlinson (12)
Belper School, Belper

Feelings I Understand

I understand,
The feelings you have,
Love and depression,
They drive you mad,
You look at him,
He looks at you,
Then you smile,
It's all you can do,
But when he's not there,
You feel so alone,
You just sit in your room,
On your own,
You try to call him,
And he's not there,
So you look at the stars,
And stare,
I know why you do this,
I know how you feel,
I ask myself the same question,
Is he for real?

Stacy-Louise Moore (16)
Belper School, Belper

My Poem

Here is my poem,
I don't know what to say,
People just going around writing them,
Each and every day.

It's not easy writing a poem,
You just can't think,
About anything in the world,
So I'm writing it in pink!

Emily Wright (13)
Frederick Gent School, South Normanton

Sheep

Sheep are really cute,
All fluffy like a cloud,
People should not eat them,
When I saw them I was wowed.

They walk around in a field,
Eating grass all day,
They always like to laze about,
They also eat hay.

So that's my poem about sheep,
I like them a lot, they're really sweet!

Kelsey Severns (12)
Frederick Gent School, South Normanton

The Footballer's Poem

Football is a dazzling game
All the players have great fame
When they get out on that pitch
They come back with a stitch

When that goal is scored
I am adored
And that's my football poem
So now I am going.

Josh Graney (12)
Frederick Gent School, South Normanton

Boxing Championships

I'm finally in the championships,
After years of training,
I hit him with some good shots,
And now he is complaining,

I'm fighting for my club,
I won't let them down,
He hits me quite hard,
Now the people have got a frown,

I come back harder in the second round,
I finally knock him down,
I duck two of his shots
And now he's the one with a frown,

Last round comes up,
I hit him with an uppercut,
Duck another shot of his,
And come round with a hook,

One judge scores the fight to me,
One judge for him,
Last one scores it to . . . *me!*
I've won, *yippee!*

Although this is just the first round,
I'm over the moon,
Me, my mum and dad are so happy,
The quarter finals are coming soon.

Ashley Greaves (13)
Frederick Gent School, South Normanton

The Untouched Rose

My eyes look on
into endless skies
forever I'll see that rose.

For skies high
and seas deep
that rose shall never sleep!

As sure as the sun
shall rise and set
in my heart
that rose is dead!

It brought a tear
to every eye
but not once
did I cry.

With the angels
fly away
I'll see you soon
come what may!

Kirsty Davis (14)
Frederick Gent School, South Normanton

Seasons Of The Year

Spring is a season not to be forgotten,
Birds chirping all the time,
Flowers blooming everywhere,
And animals being born.

Summer is here,
Holidays away,
The school year's ended,
The fun begins.

Autumn is arriving,
The school year starts,
There are not many birds,
Instead there are uniforms with children in.

Winter is cold,
There's snow all about,
You know it's Christmas time,
Because Santa's out.

These are the seasons of the year,
They come around and cheer up your year.

Rhianna Kean (11)
Frederick Gent School, South Normanton

Crime

Getting a kick,
Out of being sick,
How bad is that,
You must feel like a rat.
From breaking into a house,
And stamping on a mouse,
To grabbing a knife,
And killing a wife,
It's all crime, right?
What's the point in starting a fight?
After all it's not very bright.
If only you had a clue,
Of all the pain you put people through.
Inside and out,
You gave them a fright.
Do you do it for their money,
Or do you just find it funny?
Are you crazy or are you mad,
Or are you actually really bad?
One last thought from me to you,
Please just think before you do!

Ashleigh Chrich (13)
Frederick Gent School, South Normanton

Me And My Mates

We meet at Briary Court every day without fail,
Whether the weather be thunder, sun, rain or hail,
It's muddy but we don't even care,
Cos all we do is play football,
Manhunt as well,
I enjoy my time on there, it's swell,
There are loads of funny things happening,
Like Joe and Josh running for the ball
And falling over a piece of rope,
Me falling over my own two feet,
Andy hitting the ball,
Breaking some poor soul's hanging basket off its hooks.
Feel sorry for the basket!
Kelsey running, falling over onto her backside
And getting covered in mud,
Scott losing his phone, trying to find it, blaming everyone he sees,
Until he finds it in his pocket!
Me again trying to skill everyone, falling over the ball,
All these things make me happy,
On Briary Court every day without fail,
Whether the weather be thunder, sun, rain or hail.

Daniel Machin (13)
Frederick Gent School, South Normanton

Evil And Good

Evil
When the sun is setting
Put in this load inside
The body of a giant toad
Put in the brain of a boar
To strengthen it up a bit more
Make it taste like hell
Then let it bubble and boil
And don't let it get spoiled.

Good
When the sun is rising
Put in a herbal remedy
The best there can be!
Do not frown, chin up
And always grin
Get a fairy and let it scream
Place in the tears
Before the animal hears
Put in sunshine
And watch evil become good again.

Keanan Wright (12)
Frederick Gent School, South Normanton

Joy

Joy is the colour orange
it tastes like pancakes
it smells like apple juice
it looks like a strawberry
it sounds like a crowd cheering
it feels like jelly.

Dominic Reeve **(12)**
Highfields School, Matlock

My Cat

He's a cat that nobody knows
He's very slick and slim
He's fast but can be slow
His claws are as sharp as knives
He's as clever as Mr Einstein
His eyes are as orange as fire
He likes to eat like a rhino
He has razor-sharp teeth
His coat is as soft as silk
His coat is black, a jet-black
While a snow is as grey as rich grey.

Luke Wainwright (12)
Highfields School, Matlock

Joy

Joy is bright blue
It tastes like chicken kebabs
It smells like perfume
It looks like a sunset over the water
It sounds like a waterfall
And it feels like a soft cat.

Dayle Minshull **(12)**
Highfields School, Matlock

Jealousy

Jealousy is green
It tastes like raw jelly
It smells like gym socks
It looks like a possessed cat
It sounds like a dog fight
It feels like a rough doorman
That's jealousy.

Danielle Walker (13)
Highfields School, Matlock

Love

Love is as bright as red
It tastes like sweet sugar
It smells like a handful of roses
It looks like feathers and wool
It sounds like birds singing in a morning
It feels warm and soft!

Andy Elder (12)
Highfields School, Matlock

The Lion

In a blue sky light
a lion awakes with a yawn
showing off his fine teeth, yet so lethal.
He stands tall and proud with confidence
like he owns the world.
He stretches, the size of a snake.
He takes his prey like taking candy from a baby.
He is as fast as a tiger yet slower than a cheetah.
His strength is phenomenal.
His claws are as strong as screws through wood
and as sharp as the point of a kitchen knife.
I wouldn't like to meet this fella.

Sam Emery (12)
Highfields School, Matlock

The Infants

My teacher was old and she was very kind.
She wore a red scarf and glasses.
I remember that she used to make us get embarrassed.
She made me feel happy because I got bored, she gave us sweets.
I loved the way that she let us go outside if we wanted to.
I hated the way that we got done for running in the nursery.
The walls were covered with paintings and stuff we did
                                          with our fingers.
In the corner there was a naughty corner where bad people
                                          were sent.

The air smelt of paint and sand, everything we did.
The playground was the best,
It had a sandpit, we played in the sandpit the whole time,
It was the best, also we got milk and cookies.
At the end of break we got sweets and lots of chocolate.
I miss infants but time moves on.

James Bailey (12)
Highfields School, Matlock

Love

Love is the colour of candy pink,
It tastes like sweet strawberry bubblegum,
It smells like cherry-flavoured fragrance,
It looks like a gleaming star at night,
It sounds like a heart beating,
It feels so right.

Adrienne Marsden (13)
Highfields School, Matlock

The Horse

The horse is black
Its neck as strong and stiff as a metal pole
It runs like a warrior
About to plough its sword into its enemy
It sleeps in a corner with wide big eyes
As proud as the Statue of Liberty.

Its hooves dong on the floor like weights dropping
Its tail swishes in the wind
Its ears as pointy as a pin top
Its fur as soft as silk
Its tail and mane are like a spider's web
It goes back into its corner and never comes back.

Beth Wild (12)
Highfields School, Matlock

Rats

Rats, big eyes like beads
Rats climb like monkeys
Rats' claws as sharp as eagles'
Rats, as fast as cheetahs
Rats burrow through sawdust as quick as a mole
Rats, clever as a three-year-old
Rats run down ropes like a plane landing
Rats sleep curled up like a hedgehog hibernating
Rats watch you like a lion watches its prey.

Bethany Allwright (12)
Highfields School, Matlock

Fear Of Homework

I came in from school with homework last night,
my teacher had given me a poem to write.
A poem about my favourite book,
this task was too hard so in my room I snook.

Out of my school clothes and on my PC,
avoiding my dad, while Mum cooks the tea.
I'd play on my PlayStation, Xbox or my PC,
hope to get out of it cos it was too hard for me.

Dad must have known I was trying to shirk,
cos then came the words, 'Have you any homework?
If you've got any homework please bring it to me,
we'll get it done before you have ya tea.'

Worried I was, while he has a look,
cos I'd got a poem to write about reading a book.
While Dad had a read, pen and jotter I get,
I wonder if we will use the Internet.

'It's not that hard, lad, so don't look so sad.'
'Well I'd feel better if you helped me, Dad.'
'With a little help, you'll soon get it right,
and if we're lucky, we'll finish it tonight.'

This homework was hard, not once we brainstormed,
then the words came flowing and the story soon formed.
With a page full of words and pen in my hand,
next to the laptop and websites we scanned.

We found www.rhymezone.com,
that's the cool Internet site, where the rhyme came from.
It didn't take too long to put all the words in a list,
then I wrote a poem with a bit of a twist.

A bit of planning, and well, sort of a vision,
helped make it easy to make the decision,
to write about a boy looking down on himself,
reading a book he took down off the shelf.

Reading his poem finally down into print,
wondering if the published poem would make him a mint.
With planning and help, we soon got it done,
well writing this poem was a lot of fun.

A poem about homework and a brainstormed idea,
something he didn't really need to worry or fear.
Bit of guidance from parents, sisters and Internet too,
you're reading this poem so is the little boy, *you?*

Ashley Waldram (11)
John Port School, Derby

A Cyberman

A steel case hides all,
hiding emotions,
hiding what's left,
its silver frame glints in the sun,
its terror is known throughout,
the metal fingers wriggle and flex,
looking for races to conquer.
If a creature meets this monster,
it becomes an obedient copy.
Metal, steel all around,
layer upon layer of snaking tubes.
Only a distant flicker of its original form,
the nightmare.
The Cyberman.

Hannah Stanworth (12)
John Port School, Derby

The Dancer

The dancer whirls around and around
Up and down
She dresses in pink
Not stopping to think
The dancer whirls around and around
Up and down
Everyone stops to know she's here
Yet everyone knows that she'll appear
The dancer whirls around and around
Up and down
Bang! Crash!
She falls on the floor
She looks at the chore
'Never more!' she says
But still
The dancer whirls
Around and around
Up and down.

Jasmin Kaur Gill (11)
John Port School, Derby

Just Say Ding-Dang-Do

If you're feeling down and feeling blue,
Just say ding-dang-do.

If you really think that everyone hates you,
Just say ding-dang-do.

If you're in the pool and you need the loo,
Just say ding-dang-do.

If your best mate is sixty-two,
Just say ding-dang-do.

Thomas Knowles (12)
Kirk Hallam Community Technology College, Ilkeston

Your Friends

Friends are always there for you
No matter what you're going through
But that's just the start.

They're there to have a laugh with
They're there to help with your problems
They're there to mess about with.

But sometimes it all goes wrong
Sometimes you have a fall out
And you feel all alone.

It's not a very nice feeling
But then it all gets better
And you're all friends again.

You feel very happy
But just remember how it feels
To be all alone.

Lucy Wishart (12)
Kirk Hallam Community Technology College, Ilkeston

Dance Show

Shake to the left
Boogie to the right
Teacher showed me
How to dance tonight

Parents were watching
Me on the stage
I've been dancing
Since a young age

I was nervous
I was scared
Bam!
I'm on.

It was fun
I liked it
I just loved
Every single bit.

Alice Clayton (12)
Kirk Hallam Community Technology College, Ilkeston

Burn, Burn

If you can't tell
this is about Hell
over here, over there
the fires are everywhere.

Burn, burn
the fires flare
you may despair
but if you go there
you won't dare.

The fiery Devil
he lives there
torturing souls
in his lair.

An arrow strikes his bare foot
the rebels have escaped their hut
they get out just like that
they got away
but he'll have them back . . . some day.

Jake Kelly-Winson (12)
Kirk Hallam Community Technology College, Ilkeston

Sir Dumbalot And The Large Dragon

In a kingdom far away
That was happy every day
Arrived a dragon, mean and large
Approached the king and said, 'I'm in charge!'
But in the midst of this distress
Was a young happy princess
This enraged the dragon quite a lot
So he took her and locked her up
Now the king was very sad
He said, 'Oh my! This is quite bad!'
So he sent the urgent news
To the soft drinks aisle in Farm Foods
And at that moment, passing through
Was a hero brave and true
Picking up the telegram
He said, while eating bread and jam
'Oh woe! Oh sorrow! I'll be helpful
I'll go and save those silly fools.'
So he rushed right out of the shop
He didn't pay, he had forgot
He jumped onto his trusty horse
And rushed right down the fastest course
After passing a huge wagon
He came to town and slayed the dragon
Freed the princess and the town
The king let him try on the crown
That's the end of my little story
At least it wasn't all that gory!

Ewan Moore (12)
Kirk Hallam Community Technology College, Ilkeston

Trojan War - Haiku

Spears wound great thick shields
Glittering swords slice the air
Great warriors dead.

Jack Middleton (12)
Kirk Hallam Community Technology College, Ilkeston

The Locked Box

Do not open the locked box, that your heart so badly desires.
The woodwork has faded yet you can still see the remains
of the people who've tried.
But I know you don't dare because . . .

Do not open the locked box, that people's hearts so badly desire.
Remains of souls and faded woodwork, people have tried before.
But I know you don't dare because . . .

Do not open the locked box, do not let your heart desire,
or it could be your soul instead.
You love the woodwork though it has faded.
You want to try but I know you don't dare because . . .

Do not open the locked box, you might think it's your heart's desire.
The people you love have faded into the woodwork.
You want to rescue them, you want to try,
But I know you don't dare because . . .

Do not open the locked box, people's hearts become your desire.
You're beginning to fade into the woodwork you once loved.
You're starting to hate the people you knew, you want to get out,
You want to be rescued.
But I thought you didn't dare . . .

Lucy Wilson (12)
Kirk Hallam Community Technology College, Ilkeston

The Brain

A teacher's brain is a marvellous thing
Although I must admit quite bizarre
With extra eyes in the back of the head
And a deadly detention radar

The only way in is a treacherous route
Not for the cowardly and weak
For what lies ahead up the dark right nostril
Is something too dreadful to speak

I hold on tight and take a left
To where I'm not quite sure
Until I reached the end of the trail
With nothing except for a drawer

I tug and tug with all my might
Until the drawer finally gives way
Inside is a stack of books and files
With test papers on display

It is then I decide to have some fun
As I could rule the school
I could decide what stays and what goes
I could even rewrite the rules

Away with science, out with maths,
Ban the dreaded PE
Wait, hold on a minute, I know what to do
Take the day off, it's fine with me!

Eleanor Partridge (13)
Kirk Hallam Community Technology College, Ilkeston

An Almost Empty Universe

A rocket blasted off from Earth
With a girl and a monkey too.

When they reach space
They can't see a thing at all.

All of a sudden a star appeared
It looked so lonely in the immense dark.

But just as soon as one had appeared
Millions gathered in the sky.

A blinding light exploded in the dark
And suddenly the girl could see.

A small blue ball flew near the light
And then an orange one followed.

The girl looked back to her home planet
Which was joined by a red rocky circle.

A giant gas ball flew into sight
With another planet with a ring.

Two colder planets adding to the line
Very soon the universe will be full!

Finally a tiny ice ball finishes it all
Now we have a solar system!

It isn't long until there is a problem
And Pluto is sent away.

And now what was a family of nine
Is now a family of eight.

So now my very easy method
Just speeds up naming . . .

The girl and the monkey too
Go home and sleep tonight.

Natalie Whitehead (12)
Kirk Hallam Community Technology College, Ilkeston

Bullying

'Please leave me alone!' the girl would say,
They'd tell her she was stupid, she wasn't special, no one cared.
She knew someone would help her,
But she could not tell a soul. She was alone.

At the weekend she could not play,
She'd sit in her room all day.
This girl would worry about the bullies,
What they'd do next, would they steal her lunch, her money,
Or what? They picked on her because she was a swot,
It was not her fault she was good at things,
But instead of praise the bullies brought,
A lot of sadness to her life.

She wondered why she was the target, why no one else?
But then she stopped wondering and started,
Being bad at everything.
But they did not stop, they carried on,
As more and more detentions built up.

But finally, after months and months,
They'd finished with her and left her alone.
And strangely she hated it, being bored and on her own,
So she made some friends and got on her feet,
The bullies however were caught by a teacher,
After a boy they'd started bullying told on them.

Eventually this girl had a big smile on her face,
And she was happy again,
She's still happy now,
Because strangely enough that girl is me!

Helen Oxbrough (12)
Kirk Hallam Community Technology College, Ilkeston

The Odyssey

An amazing film I just watched
Snuggled upon the sofa.
An adventure story it was
Full of lots of long journeys.

Now I have to make one myself
Dragging myself away from the TV.
I make for the on/off button
The late night TV blaring away.

With the last of my energy
I head for the door.
Between the living room and hall
Its great length is scary.

Then the millions of stairs
Towering above me.
I step on the first one
Only twelve more to go.

The top is nearing sight
Only a few more metres to go.
The bedroom door is closed
More energy to be wasted.

Leaning on the rail
I drag myself to the door.
At last I open the door
And fall onto the cloud that is my bed.

Craig Reeve (13)
Kirk Hallam Community Technology College, Ilkeston

Haikus

Death met them at Troy
Hector slayed Greeks for his boy
Priam watched, smiling.

Their names shall live on
Until the final sun sets
On time and on life.

Alex Simpson (12)
Kirk Hallam Community Technology College, Ilkeston

Bad Parents

I was like a child to you,
That you loved and cared for.
You said you would look after me,
Do you love me anymore?

You pulled my ear, sat on my tail,
Hardly ever remembered to feed me.
You called me names like 'stupid dog',
In every way you hurt me.

This carried on for many years,
You probably don't regret,
That those six years of my life,
I will never forget.

Then one day I was saved,
In a way some think of as bad.
I died that day, on June the first,
And to be honest I was glad.

You shed no tear of mourning,
You were glad to see me go.
I'm much happier with my new family,
Watching you down below.

Ruth Webster (11)
Landau Forte College, Derby

School Misses

Different lectures,
Busy playground,
Watching people play,
Getting hurt,
Learning new things,
Doing concerts and plays,
Winning races,
Getting prizes,
Some teachers, really scary,
Going on trips,
Having fun,
Come back to school.

Having friends is the best prize of all,
We stand together strong and tall.

Makhan Manraj Singh Johal (11)
Landau Forte College, Derby

The Normal School Day

Different friends
Passing notes
Some are really unfunny jokes.

Pupils crying
Teachers shouting
Surprised there isn't even a clouting.

Work, work, work
Work all day
But sometimes we do get to play.

Really good work
Equals many sweets
Oh, I do sure love these treats.

The school bell rings
Have a little roam
Then it is certainly time to go home.

Kelly Harland (11)
Landau Forte College, Derby

Remember That?

Making new friends,
Passing long notes,
Teachers driving you round the bend,
Lots of dos and don'ts.

Lunchtime blessed,
Break time overrated,
What test?
High hopes deflated.

Wishing good luck,
What will you do after,
Clean up that muck!
The sound ringing through the hall is laughter.

School ties thrown away,
Detentions kept at bay,
Goodbye to you,
Goodbye to me,
I'll miss you all dearly!

(Remember that . . . last year?)

Ariel Draper (11)
Landau Forte College, Derby

School Memories

Starting school at 9.30,
Running round the corridors,
Shouting, screaming,
Passing by all the teachers
Saying, 'Bye!'
Christmas, playing up,
Where is Mary and the lamb?
Friends always there
When you are down,
Half are playing clowns.

Sharna Farrar (11)
Landau Forte College, Derby

School Sucks

School is super boring
Everyone is snoring
Everyone thinks school sucks
We all hate the books
Teachers shouting and balling
And boys screaming after scoring
What fun we had
Yet everything was too long
Home time has come.

James Pittham (11)
Landau Forte College, Derby

School Days

All my friends making me laugh
School trips were never naff,
Writing stories was always fun
Bad playtime games, we always got done.

Playing for tag rugby and football team
New football boots, shiny and clean,
Covered in mud when we got cropped
Getting out of breath from shouting a lot.

Teacher's jokes, never funny
When we're inside, it's always sunny,
Dinner times were always cool
But I will never forget playing Frustration
On the last day of school!

William Glasby (11)
Landau Forte College, Derby

My Primary School

In my school we used to have fun
and we used to play water fights with water guns.
I had a fight with my friend.
I pushed him on a fence.
He started to bleed and was about to tell Miss Stence
and then I stopped him telling Miss Stence by giving him 50 pence!
Rooms and rooms all around the school.
Some people think they're bad and cool.

Rafi Riaz (11)
Landau Forte College, Derby

School Memories

The sound of the school bus coming down the street.
Children shouting as they get off the bus.
Boys fighting over a game of football.
And girls fighting over boys.
Teachers in the staffroom having a gossip.
Teachers approach the playground
Whistle goes, everything quiet
Children settling down, getting on with work
And getting ready for hard days, days of work,
Sums, words and spellings.
End of school time, children scream with joy.
Children gone home from school
Quiet, teachers gone,
School closed, waiting until next morning!

Sarah Finan (12)
Landau Forte College, Derby

School Memories

Teachers are scary,
Detention's cruel,
Children screaming,
School's not cool!

Children's eyes on the clock,
Then the bell rings,
'Fire bell children!'
Girls run out giggling,
Boys run out screaming with laughter,
It was just a drill!

Off to work,
Everyone sighs,
Then, last few minutes of quiet
And then a last bell,
Home time!

Georgia Watson (11)
Landau Forte College, Derby

Memories From School

My first year there was really good
as I walked into the toilet I saw a massive flood.
In PE I was named The Cricket King
because I used to send the ball flying with one hell of a swing.
I remember when my team won the football competition
it was our biggest ambition.
I remember on sports day when my team won
I will remember that day forever, it was so fun.
I remember when it was Easter awards
my friend Joseph was always bored.
Well it wouldn't have been very fun when you received none
there's no wonder he was always looking glum
when it used to come.
The best time of all is when me and my friends
used to stand, strong and tall.

Kurtis O'Sullivan (11)
Landau Forte College, Derby

My Old School

My four teachers
Scary and tall
Apart from Ms Blurton
She is really small.

The head teacher shouting
On school sports day
Year 3s coming up to us
Wanting to play.

School dinner's manky
Mashed potato slush
Dead flies in the salad
Pudding's absolutely lush.

School council meetings
Nearly every week
Moaning teachers telling you
When and when not to speak.

Sophie Middleton (11)
Landau Forte College, Derby

Old School

Scrabble, scrabble over toys
Scrabble, scrabble over boys
No more scrabble over toys
No more scrabble over boys
No more scrabble because we've moved
Now it is shouting, screaming in the school
Running down the corridor
People groaning, teacher moaning.

Charli Blurton (11)
Landau Forte College, Derby

Year Six Memories

Children. Eager, dashing around.
Race into school, when the bell sounds.
Everywhere's silent as assembly begins.
Listening intently to the teacher's din.

We troop up to the classroom,
Thinking about the day's first lesson.
Wow! It's art! Time to get messy.
Oh no! Next is maths - we have a problem
But soon it's home time - at last, relaxation.

Alexandra Duesbury (11)
Landau Forte College, Derby

Space Travel

S pace travel is wonderful,
P erfect way to see the world,
A hop in a spaceship,
C an get you to Mars,
E veryone can get the ticket to go,

T here is a space for everyone,
R ight now is the time for you,
A real adventure,
V enus is the planet for me,
E nding is coming now,
L anding, what a trip!

Alex Withey (12)
Landau Forte College, Derby

The Definition of Celebrity

C ool and posh mostly
E ating lots of food
L urking around with money
E xcited to meet you
B eautiful on the outside
R ough on the inside
I nternationally known and wanted
T ime is something that flies
Y ikes! That's the definition of . . . *celebrity!*

Bhavan Chahal (11)
Landau Forte College, Derby

A Random Course Of Events

A chair and a table,
That had three legs,
Landed on a turtle,
Who had just laid its eggs.
A fresh stack of ham,
Floated through waters murky,
An old man drove past,
On his way to Albuquerque.
Miners dig under,
A plane flies overhead,
A man jumps out,
And lands on his bed.
These words of wisdom I dispense,
On the off chance any of this made sense.

Chris Brown (17)
Landau Forte College, Derby

War Of Our World

Oh moon, oh stars, shining so bright
Stop all the bloodshed happening tonight
It started, it stopped, but started again
No one is stopping it, not even the UN
We see them cry, before babies are killed
We see them pray, before blood is spilled
Fathers fight whilst mothers weep
Bodies unknown are buried so deep
Oh moon, oh stars, shining so bright
Listen to my words, stop the fight.

Salma Moghal (17)
Landau Forte College, Derby

Flat-Pack Living

Smart living saves money
Life begins at home
Take control of your things
Chuck out the chintz
Fabric from £1.59 a metre
See page 142 then go to the store for more
Klippan sofa, Ektorp Jenylund armchair
Billy bookcase, Bettan Blom cushion
Lack lamp

Afford what you need today
Get it now
Time to focus on your world
New autumn feelings
Pölarvide throws from £2.59
See page 189 then go to the store for more
Lycksele sofa bed, Skruvsta swivel armchair
Norrebo bookcase, Tylösand removable covers
Vasen vase

Check often for new products and new ideas
Quick-fix furniture
It's OK to change your mind
Take home a taste of Sweden
Meatballs with cream sauce and linngonberry jam £2.75
Mysinge corner sofa, Solsta Pällbo footstool
Effectiv bookcase, Bibbi Snurr single quilt cover
Kristaller chandelier

See page 194 then go to the store for more.

Chloe Tomlinson (18)
Landau Forte College, Derby

Actress (4.2.06)

A gothic dig was the place we met
Your coat smelt of perfume and cigarettes
You came across in your own drunken trance
My God, I am thankful that you didn't see me dance
I had never felt so glad to be taken by the hand
For no one else thinks it, you're the finest in the land
I had yearned for an angel, and that night I didn't fail
Just a pity something so heavenly, was in truth betrayal
Yeah, I left you on the debris, that's not so hard to see
But I wonder, we will see each other - before the sky turns green?

Alfie Wilson (17)
Landau Forte College, Derby

Timeless . . .

Just like a bird flying through the sky,
Way up high,
Just like the sun, falling to the west,
I know you best,
Just like the sea crashing on the shore,
I love you more.

The moon, rising across the night sky,
Will never die,
The Earth, circling the sun,
Will never be done,
The rain, falling across the plain,
Will never wane,
Just as my love for you,
Will never be through.

Heather Richardson (17)
Landau Forte College, Derby

Brief Flower

She is the flower of the night,
The endless fog, the biting chill.
The silent cloud without delight,
The sunken shadow on the hill.

My thunder's grace she came to fill,
Memories now faded, motives now lost.
But broken hearts, she brought us nil,
The blooded hand, the endless cost

Of dark's despair, of morning's frost.
In hope of freedom, sight of freedom,
Frozen dreams of minds embossed
With words of fury; sorrow's wisdom.

Yet once again the morning comes,
Night's blanket forced into retreat,
The shadows blinded, dark succumbs,
To hide again, her work complete.

The flower dies, the people mourn
The revolution, dead and gone.

Barnaby Lane (17)
Landau Forte College, Derby

Red Line

I see the red line start to grow;
Weaving patterns to and fro;
Setting the canvas ablaze with fire,
Cutting through the skin entire.
Intricate patterns materialise,
Like the webs of lies I despise.
My mask of joy has departed
And my revenge has just started.
Out pours all my steaming hate,
Today there will be no debate!
Everything is oh so very clear
And in my heart I have no fear.
Soon the red begins to flow,
Like a river that's oh so slow.
Twisting through my work of art,
Slicing up my empty heart.
And as my soul ebbs away,
I think of what I did today;
I killed the thing I hated most.
I lift my glass, a final toast.
You just don't understand the glee
That I get from killing me.

Heidi Rudge (17)
Landau Forte College, Derby

The Cats Next Door

The cat next door is called Basil Brush
He is orange with four little white paws
His eyes are green with a pink nose.

Chippie is his brother, also with white paws
The two cats play together
Chippie and Basil are friends for evermore.

Jamie Woodside (11)
Lees Brook Community Sports College, Derby

Dogs

Dogs are daring, dangerous all,
like to jump off the garden wall,
jumping, crashing then they fall.

Getting up, slow as a snail,
carrying on because it's fun,
the owner comes so they run.

Lauren Decosta (11)
Lees Brook Community Sports College, Derby

The Proud Peacock

The proud peacock struts round the garden,
as royal as a king.
Showing off his brightly coloured feathers,
they really are amazing.
Even though he cannot fly,
he doesn't seem to care.
He's too busy fanning his up into the air.
Blues and greens so bright they shine,
they look like lots of eyes staring straight into mine.
He looks so majestic, so superior and brave
as he poses to the lady peacocks
and fans his feathers to wave.

Heather Slater (11)
Lees Brook Community Sports College, Derby

Little Robin

There's a robin on my window sill,
I think it wants some bread,
So I creep into the kitchen and get half a slice instead.

It pecks at the crumbs,
Ruffles its wings in my direction
And dives off into the trees.

So I sit here quite lonely,
Until tomorrow night,
When I see the bird again, what a lovely sight.

Laura Duxbury (11)
Lees Brook Community Sports College, Derby

The Parrot

She flies through jungles, quick in flight,
Her feathers coloured oh so bright,
A coloured gem in moonlight,
Flapping wings with all her might,
Squawking loud and proud tonight, yes,
She flies through jungles quick in flight.

Maddison Ginn (12)
Lees Brook Community Sports College, Derby

The King Of The Pride

The tiger watched his prey at night
With concentrated beady eyes.
He stalked his prey till time was right
Then pounded on it with all his might.

He tore his meat with teeth so deep
Then dragged his meat to his lair.
With the rest of the pride giving a stare
He stood tall and proud.
Then turned to the crowd
With his head held high, he roared so loud.

He is the king of the pride.

Taylor Stark (12)
Lees Brook Community Sports College, Derby

My Cat

I have a cat, her name is Maizy.
My friends think that she is crazy.
In the sun she lies all day long.

Like a tiger she is very strong.
Prowling in the grass for her prey.
Catching mice and sleeping after play.

Daniel Wilkinson
Lees Brook Community Sports College, Derby

The Shadow

He's stuck to me day and night,
But only shows up in the light,
He copies me as you'll see,
I wave to him, he waves to me,
It does not ever matter who,
He will always be waiting for you.

Lisa Miller (12)
Lees Brook Community Sports College, Derby

The Old Car

I was a car racing down the road
Once I was all shiny and red
I was waiting to be driven
My wheels were all black and clean
My windows were spotless
So you could see through them
But now I am just the same old vehicle
All rusty and dull
Nobody ever rides in me anymore
My windows are covered with dust
Soon I will be sitting in a rusty garage
All dark and lonely.

Amy Cropley
Lees Brook Community Sports College, Derby

The Car

I am an old race car
Once I raced along the race track
Breaking world records
Stopping hearts of fans
That bet on other cars
So shiny was my coat of red
Made other cars drop down dead
Minibuses watched and stared
While coaches simply stopped and glared
But now I am a bit of metal
Never am I used
My body is broken into bits
While my heart breaks.
Soon I am to be taken in
By a man to be raced again.

Antonia Watts (12)
Lees Brook Community Sports College, Derby

Hamster

He grabs the side of his cage with tiny paws,
he climbs through the maze of multicoloured tubes
and scurries around, hoarding his food in secret places.

He sleeps, he drinks, he eats, he plays,
all the way from dusk until dawn.

Samuel Kohrs (12)
Lees Brook Community Sports College, Derby

My Animal Poem

I am a dog running round the fields
Chasing a stick and a ball.
When I'm tired I go home without my owner
Because he could stay out all night.
When he comes home he gets me a drink
And something to eat and that's what happens every day
Because he's the best owner ever and I love him.
I hope he never leaves.

Ryan Fitzhugh (12)
Lees Brook Community Sports College, Derby

Snake

The snake slithers through the grass
All the others stare as he passes
They're all quite frightened to see him there
Lions, tigers and even the bears.

There are lots of different species of snakes
Anacondas you'll find down in the lakes
Some live in trees, others on the ground
Some have bright colours and one a rattling sound.

Callum Thompson (12)
Lees Brook Community Sports College, Derby

The Lion

He runs around giving great big roars,
He opens his mouth as you see his jaws,
And he jumps in the air with his crooked claws.

He is tired from the mighty sun's rays,
So he goes to sleep in some ginger hay,
Ready to play another day.

Zavier Hobby (12)
Lees Brook Community Sports College, Derby

A Tale Of An Old Steam Train

I am an old steam train
Once I ferried thousands
With my plume of thick steam
All mankind seemed to love me.

They loved to see me travel
My big and powerful engines
Were so strong
My speed blinded trainspotters
As they ate their sarnies and drank their coffee.

But now I do not hiss
My engine has frozen
My funnel is bent
And my pistons have snapped.

But my future is not all doom and gloom
Soon I will be cleaned and polished
I will be classed as an antique.

Charlie Torry (13)
Lees Brook Community Sports College, Derby

My Trainer

I am an Adidas trainer

Once I was at the height of fashion
and the pride of every boy's life
a boy was weird if he didn't have me
or one of my family.
I would run past my Umbro cousins
and my Nike brothers
my blue stripes were washed till they shone
my laces would fly in the breeze.

But now my colours are faded
my laces are gone
my grip is loosened
and my value is down.

But soon there is hope
just maybe
just maybe
I will run again.

Christopher Swain (12)
Lees Brook Community Sports College, Derby

Creature

Once upon a stormy night
There was a creature out of sight
Not harmful to you and me
Not even harmful to the sea
Walk around the house to the back
There was the creature in a sack
The creature must have been so sad
The man who did this must be mad
He came home every day
And hit the creature anyway
So now you know well and true
Go tell your friends as I did to you.

Michael Toryusen (12)
Lees Brook Community Sports College, Derby

The Brick Game Boy

I am an old brick Game Boy
Once I was wanted all over the land
The children asked for me for weeks and weeks
But now I gather dust, I am not wanted
The children hate me but at least now I know
I won't be the only one in the drawer,
Soon I will die, my battery will fade
And I will be sold for very little.

Adam Taylor (12)
Lees Brook Community Sports College, Derby

The Teddy Bear

I am an old teddy bear,
Once I was cuddled,
Loved and cared for,
I lived in a big warm house,
With a caring little girl,
Everyone adored me,
I had neat and tidy fur,
People always wanted me,
When they visited my family,
But now I'm all alone,
With a dustbin for a home,
The little girl's grown up now,
And left me on my own,
Soon the dustbin van will come,
And take me away from this place.

Lauren Sayers (12)
Lees Brook Community Sports College, Derby

My Poem About The Old Person

I am an old person
once I was full of life
willing to do activities
and I was as happy as could be
but now I am weak
and I have no more strength
I can hardly move
and I hurt, in pain all over
soon I think I will die
and go in to peace
into my cold, lonely grave
and I will look over my family
from within my heart and Heaven.

Charlotte Wilkinson (12)
Lees Brook Community Sports College, Derby

The Old Motorbike

I am an old Norton Commando motorbike
Once I ripped up the roads with a reckless abandon
My polished chrome petrol tank glistening in the sun.
My owner thought my worth was priceless.
He spent time and effort on me without complaint
I was king of the road
Nobody could beat me, get close to me
As I streaked past like a bullet
But now I'm rotting behind an old shed
My tyres are bald
My petrol tank corroded
My spirit is crushed
Soon I will rise like a phoenix from the ashes.

Alex Nuttall (12)
Lees Brook Community Sports College, Derby

Untitled

Dozing off again on the floor,
Father is pouring a drink, gagging for more.
I hit the floor and fall asleep,
without a mattress or a sheet.

I wake in the morning,
as the sun is dawning.
I feel the pain in my head,
I just want to lie in bed.

The water in my mouth,
could get us out of this drought.
But my stomach is aching,
with the smell of Nana baking.

The woman is coming over tonight,
not much to my father's delight.
I hope she takes me away this time,
because life here is barely fine.

But time for school,
remember to follow that rule.
Run all the way home,
can't stay alone.

Elisabeth Sproat (12)
Lees Brook Community Sports College, Derby

A Dog's Life

Why was I born into a horrible place?
No one to play with, no ball to chase,
Being chained up with nowhere to go,
Sitting in the rain, lying in the snow,
Why do these men make me always fight,
Then watch me bleed most of the night?
I can't remember the last time I was fed,
But they remember how to kick me in the head.
I wish I could run away and be free,
And find someone who could really love me,
But here I am, another kick to the head,
I can't stand my life, I'd rather be dead.

Jack Leverington (12)
Lees Brook Community Sports College, Derby

Mistreated Bear

I feel so sad and alone,
Being made to sing and dance,
If only I couldn't talk
And just be normal like every other bear.

The children all sing along
And laugh and point at me,
But then they realise how sad I am
And complain about how I have been mistreated.

I feel so used and abused,
For people's entertainment.
But at last now I am free,
To run around as I please.

Jonny Miles (12)
Lees Brook Community Sports College, Derby

The Old TV

I am an old television,
Once I was always used,
I was always being watched,
I was the 'new big thing'.
No TV was as good as me!
I had the best signal, best colour,
Best satellite system ever!
When it was me up against the other TVs
I always dazzled the most!
But now there's a new TV in town,
Supposedly better than me!
Better colour and everything, the whole lot!
I'm left here to break,
My TV is not being watched anymore, I'm a mess.
Soon I will be taken away, I do not know where to,
I could be cut up or hopefully go
To somewhere where I'm wanted!

Nicola Hall (12)
Lees Brook Community Sports College, Derby

Rag Doll

I am a rag doll.
Once I was a lovely little dolly,
with a pretty pink flowery brolly,
I used to have a really good friend,
but now I drive her round the bend,
I want to look good and clean,
but my old best friend is turning quite mean,
now she won't even let me shine,
she used to but now it's like committing a crime,
when she has no friends again,
she'll play with me - but that's when?
Soon I will have back my buddy,
but for now I'll have to stay muddy.
I want to be a lovely little dolly.

Karla Craven (12)
Lees Brook Community Sports College, Derby

Once I Was . . .

I am a diamond ring,
Once I was shiny and shimmering,
I was silvery-blue
With a wonderful glow.
I was shined every day
And you could see yourself
In all of my segments.
But now I am rusty
And my colour is orangey red,
My diamond is not shiny at all,
With every segment flaking away.
Soon I will be just a piece of dust,
To be thrown away
And never to be worn again.

Charlotte Hickford (12)
Lees Brook Community Sports College, Derby

Concorde

I am a Concorde.
Once I used to soar to great heights,
Breaking the speed of sound,
And people's eardrums!
Once I was the daddy of the planes,
Better than the Boeing,
I was faster than the fighter jets.
People used to pay money just to ride on me.
But now I am nothing,
Nothing but a heap of scrap metal,
My cold, mechanical heart throbbing,
I'm the last of the Concordes to be destroyed,
Soon my meaningless little life will be over.
I'll be turned into drink cans, wheel rims,
Maybe I'll be part of another plane,
They'll be happy and full of glee,
Soon they'll become worthless,
And become another destroyed plane like me.

Adam Smith (12)
Lees Brook Community Sports College, Derby

School Objects

I am aching and hurting all over,
As I kept banging against the wall,
Then this boy came, I shouted, 'No Rover!'
But it was too late, I had to cry and call,
I was gasping for air like a burst ball.

I am sitting here on the shelf,
I am frightened, lonely and freezing cold,
But now I feel like I'm shrinking as small as an elf,
Soon I'm going to be turning 50 years old,
Once I was young and new,
I wish I was like those other books too.

I am the oldest window here,
Cracked and bleeding in pain,
Once there was nothing wrong with me apart from a smear,
But now I'm falling apart in the rain,
Soon I will feel just empty and plain.

Alisha Roberts (12)
Lees Brook Community Sports College, Derby

Jet

I am an old worn out jet plane
Once I flew from Finland to Australia.
My paint job was all new and colourful.
My wings glistened in the fresh air.
My engine was all clean and new.
I couldn't complain,
I looked like a collector's item.
I was that beautiful
But now I look like a pile of junk.
My wings have lost their glistening shine.
They are all worn out and rusted.
My paint job is now grey and dull.
My engine is rubbish, I break down a lot.
I can't even get from Ireland to England.
Soon I will be cut and chopped up.
I bet I will be transformed into a new jet.
I hope I will be better in the future than now.

Oliver Bryan (12)
Lees Brook Community Sports College, Derby

Dog

She eats and drinks
She makes a noise
She is big and hairy
Like a bear.

She hates my cats
Who are two years old
She loves playing with the ball
All day and night.

Daniel Johnston (12)
Lees Brook Community Sports College, Derby

Easy Chair

I am an easy chair
But now I am a wooden clothes horse,
Everyone puts their clothes on me.
But once people used to stop and stare
And sit on me and read their books on me.
But now I wish they'd take me to the tip.
The rickety-rockety car is very slow.
They put me in their car
Thank God, my blessing's in going to the tip.
Goodbye to my family,
Goodbye to my home,
Slosh over to the side, I'm crushed.

Emily Stills (12)
Lees Brook Community Sports College, Derby

Animal Poem

My rabbit is white and grey,
She eats a carrot every day.
She's harmless and scared of cats,
She's only 3 and she's not fat.
She's called Lotty, I love her name,
She plays with me at a game.

At night she thumps her cage all night,
And wakes us up and gave us a fright.
When she bangs we can hear,
We need to sleep and close our ears.
There was a bat flying near here
And a cat that moves without fear.

Sally Iceton (12)
Lees Brook Community Sports College, Derby

The Lonely Dog

The dog is out in the cold and wet,
She was kicked out for being a bad pet.
She is out in the wind and rain,
Her owners said she was a pain.

Now she's lonely in the streets,
Looking up at the people she meets,
They say 'shoo' or 'go away',
All she wants is to play.

She was starving, hunting for food,
She hated it when she was shooed.
She looked up and barked in the sky,
Hoping a lover would walk right by.

He didn't come by later that day,
But he came one day in May.
He took her in and fed her well,
The dog had a story she wanted to tell.

The dog was named Little Fat Minnie
Even though she was quite skinny.
Now she is fattening up
And she thinks, *I'm one lucky pup.*

Daniel Caterer (12)
Lees Brook Community Sports College, Derby

The Cheetah

The cheetah runs like lightning,
Through the night and as the day is brightening.

It catches up with every animal,
Killing and thrashing like a dangerous cannibal.

It pounces on the smaller prey,
And that is the dinner for the rest of that day.

Zenna Rhodes (11)
Lees Brook Community Sports College, Derby

Little Robin

A little robin calls and wakes me
every frosty morning.
I watch him fly down from the trees
and land upon the lawn.

He folds his wings and looks around
his little eyes shine bright.
He puffs his crimson-red chest up
and sings with all his might.

Bethany Mullins (11)
Lees Brook Community Sports College, Derby

My Dolphin Friend

If I were you my dolphin friend
I would splash and splosh
If I were you my dolphin friend
In sea I'd never be lost.

If I were you my dolphin friend
I would love to swim
And when there was a swimming race
I would always win.

Why are you sad my dolphin friend?
You know I'm by your side.
Do cheer up my dolphin friend
There's no need to cry.

Why should you weep my dolphin friend?
You know I'm here for you.
We're friends forever dolphin friend
What I say is true.

Sophie Weston (11)
Sir Jonathan North Community College, Leicester

Daffodils

I wandered alone, as free as a bird
Through the serene, scenic hills
Isolated in a heavenly place,
A spectacular view before me.

Lonely strolling, dodging the trees
A primrose pool of light above,
Clumps of moss strangled my feet,
The trees swaying in the breeze.

As a cloud drifted above my head,
A gleaming glow emerged,
Glistening vibrant colours,
A scent of sweetness in the air.

Fluttering and dancing daffodils
Swaying peacefully in the breeze,
A mass of dazzling yellow heads
Surrounded by lush green grass.

A host of golden daffodils right before my eyes,
Singing gently to the whirls of the breeze,
Swirling and twirling with the golden leaves,
In the blazing sunlight.

Ellie Wightman-Bragg (11)
Sir Jonathan North Community College, Leicester

The Cat And The Runaway Bottle

I was in India.
It was dark,
everybody was asleep,
I awoke and started to cry.
My uncle awoke,
taking tired, slow steps he reached the kitchen
And he looked everywhere for my bottle,
in the cupboards, on the shelves, even the floor!
I had caused a huge racket,
crying the whole night.
My uncle finally gave up.
He ran down to the local shop,
bought a bottle.
Soon I got some warm milk,
he was relieved to see me sleep again.
In the morning my mum went into the garden,
she saw the cat,
sucking the nib of the bottle.
She was horrified.
No cat has ever entered the house since that day.

Asma Daud (11)
Sir Jonathan North Community College, Leicester

My Embarrassing Memory

Standing at the back of the assembly hall,
a singing assembly,
I got in trouble for laughing,
at the song - well it was about mice and cats.

Then had to sing another song,
whilst we were singing the lights were switched off,
so we could see the words
on the projector more clearly.

I don't know how, but by mistake,
I switched the lights on,
every single pair of eyes
were staring at me.

'Oh no,'
how embarrassing!

Mariyah Zamakda (11)
Sir Jonathan North Community College, Leicester

Primary School

It is my first day of primary school.
I am walking to my new classroom,
One hand in my pocket, the other holding my bag.
We are walking through the main hall which is filled
                            with Christmas decorations.

It seems like everything is going in slow motion.
Even my heart seems to be beating slowly.
My ears are ringing with the loudness of my heartbeat.

The head teacher who is walking with us opens the decorated door.
Everyone looks at me.
The head teacher talks to the class.
They carry on looking at me like how a wolf looks
                            when another animal crosses its territory.

I fear the worst.
I am scared that I will become a toy that they can play with,
That they can bully.
I will probably become one of those loners,
Destined to wander the playground for the rest of my school days.

It is lunchtime and everyone really likes me.
They say that I have a strange sense of humour.
I am really happy.

A month later and you would expect me to have at least one friend.
Wrong. I am wandering the playground on my own,
It's like I predicted. Maybe things will be different
                            in secondary school.

Asha Hoddoon (11)
Sir Jonathan North Community College, Leicester

Stabbed!

I was in my house,
When somebody knocked on the door.
My mum's friend Samantha.
They hurried into the kitchen.
As I entered I saw a knife on the floor.
I picked it up and put it on the kitchen surface.
It directly fell down.
Ouch!
It left a little mark.
My mum picked me up,
Put me on the kitchen surface -
Thinking of what she could do.
I started crying,
My mum quickly sprinkled tea powder.
Phew! It stopped hurting.
It was like magic.
'Tea powder stops bleeding,'
Said my dad.

Sumaiyah Walilay (11)
Sir Jonathan North Community College, Leicester

The Zip Line

Hands on the handles.
I lift my feet.
I speed down the zip line
Clinging to the bars
Faster and faster.

The wind in my hair
I focus on the way in front
The end.
I jolt and my head flings forward
I hit the cold, smooth metal of the swing
I'm in pain.

My head throbs
I drop down onto the floor
I want to cry
But I hide my face
I'm dizzy.

A tear falls down my cheek,
I blush.
I say I feel sick and my mum comforts me.
She doesn't realise why I really cry.

Why?
Why do I not tell them what happened?
No.
It will remain a secret
I grit my teeth and bear it.

I give in.
I tell my mum what is really bothering me.
She hugs me.
Now I'm OK.

Hester Dishman (11)
Sir Jonathan North Community College, Leicester

When I Fell Off A Chair

My mum was cooking in the slimy kitchen.
I was eating.
I fell off a slimy chair like a slug.
I got hurt on my lips.
When my mum saw me she was shocked.
She called my dad.
As quickly as a cheetah they took me to the smelly hospital.
I had three stitches and they really hurt.

Anisha Sattar (11)
Sir Jonathan North Community College, Leicester

My Ankle

It is a sunny summer's day
I try to see how high I can jump
Off the climbing frame
Ist bar
2nd bar
Easy peasy
3rd bar
Getting harder
4th bar
I am Olympic champion
5th bar
I'm Superman
Flying
Falling
Ow!
I land on my foot
I start to cry
Cry
Cry
Mum and Dad come
What happened?
I say how my foot hurts
A few minutes later
The shock has gone
My foot went
Zap!
When it came down
I go to hospital
An X-ray is taken of it
My ankle is sprained.

Paloma Styles (11)
Sir Jonathan North Community College, Leicester

Christmas Time

Christmas time is coming,
Snowflakes on the ground,
Jingle bells are ringing,
What a lovely sound.

Christmas time is coming,
Presents under the tree,
Lots of jelly and ice cream,
Just for you and me.

Christmas time is coming,
Santa's on his way,
To visit girls and boys,
On this special day.

Christmas time is coming,
Everywhere covered in snow,
Everybody's laughing,
Ho, ho, ho!

Alice Neal (11)
Sir Jonathan North Community College, Leicester

Whole New Place For Me

This place is so different for me
and it's difficult to get round,
but it's a wondrous place to be.
I feel so new, like a shooting star
it is such a good place to be.
I wish I could spend all my time here.
The special place I will tell soon.
My head will always be here.
Have you guessed?
Soon all will be revealed so hold on tight.
I love this place, my ideas get better here,
so I do my homework here.
Yes, it is my bedroom.

Charlotte Bailey (11)
Sir Jonathan North Community College, Leicester

Deep Blue Sea

The fishes swim,
with their twins,
under the deep blue sea.

As the sharks glide,
I slide on my slide,
under the deep blue sea.

When the whales stomp past us,
I do not fuss,
under the deep blue sea.

I am a dolphin, what else can I be?
I sit here under the old gum tree,
I live under the deep blue sea.

Sian Vaja (11)
Sir Jonathan North Community College, Leicester

Me

Some people say it comes naturally,
Some people say it's a gift.
Others say it's from their side,
And some just smile and shift.
When I'm on stage I'm all smiles,
I know they'll all fall for my act,
But when I'm at home I'm exhausted,
My mum says I should give it the sack.

Molly Carr (11)
Sir Jonathan North Community College, Leicester

An Amazing Identity

Ethnic cultures, cosmopolitan communities,
A mixture of old and a mixture of new,
A chance to show individuality, responsibility and cooperation.
That's why this poem is for you . . .

Cultivated cities and historic buildings, an identity for a certain city,
A mixture of good and a sight of the bad, proof of individuality.
We are a build up of bricks, mortar and water deep
                    within our individual bodies.
Cities standing 3D in front of one another
                like a postcard that moves into reality,
We have an identity.
Whether our hands are black or white our sense of skill is universal,
Our eyes reach out for the goodness and yearn for the truth,
A sense of complication rumbles inside our minds.
We have an identity.

Personalities and originalities all belong in the same category,
An identity.
We can be different but we all feel the same feelings,
We all want to be loved and cherished.
Differences are what make us such a warm community;
We give the different a chance to speak out.
But the truth is, there is not one person in the world that is the same,
Our faces might move and our lips might all talk,
But our feelings and thoughts are completely different.
This is the unique factor. What we all need to understand and praise.
Our identity might be hidden beneath same beliefs
But within the soul is where the identity really shows.
Don't be afraid to let the world know of yourself,
You're different to me, to your friends and everyone around you,
Your identity is an amazing factor that only you have.
We should all cherish our individual identity and speak out;
Our mouths may be the same form but our lips only
                        conjure up separate thoughts.
Thank you.

Laura Butler (13)
Sir Jonathan North Community College, Leicester

A Day In The Life Of Christopher Boone

He sits.
I sit.
He groans irrationally then hits the nearest helper
My sandwiches had pickle instead of lettuce on them
But pickle was yesterday's sandwich
He continues as if nothing has happened.
After I hit the man I remembered what adults do when this happens
He called him a little sod
Which I didn't like because I'm not little
He didn't like being punched
Just like the policeman
And just like how I didn't like being touched.
But I'm not surprised because he is sitting on a napkin
The weirdo.

I don't like public places,
That's why I sat on a square paper napkin
My name is Christopher and I have Asperger's.
I'm not like other children.
I'm different.

Charlotte King (13)
Sir Jonathan North Community College, Leicester

Asperger's

There are 13 pins - 13 pins on the floor.
Red and yellows mingling.
I yell and yell for the 13 drawing pins to be saved.
The red ones.
People stare. People laugh.
They do not even seem to standing in awe.
They say I am abnormal
But to me red and yellow pins touching
Is the thing that means the world is not normal.
Not normal. Not normal at all.

The man with the lopsided eyebrows asks again
                                    and again and again.
He gets louder and louder.
Drumming the words into me
Though I know however many times he says them,
                              I will never understand.
As it has been drummed into me enough times now
That I'm not normal. Not normal.
Not at all.

Zoë Halse (13)
Sir Jonathan North Community College, Leicester

Roses Are Red

Roses are red
Violets are blue
Sugar is sweet
But not as sweet as you.

Roses are red
Violets are blue
You don't love me
As much as I do you.

Roses are red
Violets are blue
No matter what
I will always love you.

Roses are red
Violets are blue
No matter what people say
I will never stop loving you.

Roses are red
Violets are blue
If you turn blue
You will always be true.

Jodie Barwell (11)
Sir Jonathan North Community College, Leicester

Operation

I went to South Africa for an operation.
A kidney operation.
The urine was going up the pipe back to my kidneys.
My parents and I stayed for three weeks in South Africa.
In hospital I had pipes around me.
My parents were so upset when the doctor told them.
He gave me a lollipop and he was so friendly.
My family was very upset, they phoned my parents every day
To say 'How is she today?'
My parents were so proud of me as I was so brave.
My father bought me a bicycle.
He taught me how to ride it.
My mother bought me a princess castle and a princess crown.
She told me I would always be her little princess.

Faaizah Meman (11)
Sir Jonathan North Community College, Leicester

Scary Stairs

I was standing on top of the stairs
Trying to go down backwards.
'Argh!'
I slipped and landed with a bang.
'Uaa, uaa, uaa!' I cried
And had a bruise on my forehead,
It isn't there anymore thank God!

Afifa Abdul Cadir (11)
Sir Jonathan North Community College, Leicester

Skegness

I got to Skegness fair,
It looked wicked.
All the rides, all the people, everything.
I could hear the people shouting, laughing, having fun.
'Come on let's go on the dodgems.'

There I was sitting in the dodgem car
Waiting for it to begin.

Then suddenly, *bang!*
Somebody had hit us from behind.
My neck pained, I couldn't move it.

I got off.
'You enjoyed that?'
'Not really.'

Then came the roller coaster.
I was sitting in the seat
Scared like anything.
Up, down, spinning around.
It was frightening, it was fast.

I jumped off
Feeling dizzy.
Then the pirate ship,
It started rocking slowly
Then it got faster and faster
Till I felt sick.

It was a great day!

Shezeen Sheikh (11)
Sir Jonathan North Community College, Leicester

The Tiny Black Cornflake

I was playing on the sofa, with my friend
When I got a sudden sharp pain
Like a needle in my eye.
I told my mum
She gave me a damp piece of cottonwool
To soothe it.
Then it was OK for a while.
But next morning I got the pain again
So off to the hospital I went with my mum.
It felt like we were waiting for years.
One nurse tried to get it out
(He said I had something in my eye)
But he couldn't get it out
I was winking too much
So we went out for lunch.
When we came back there was a different nurse
He got it out.
Yeah!
He said it looked like a tiny black cornflake.
I'll never play on the sofa again!

Tabitha Thompson (11)
Sir Jonathan North Community College, Leicester

Disneyland

I woke up and heard an ear-splitting row
Asked my mum why it had commenced and how
I was told we were going to a place called Disneyland
However, I had to be good and give her a helping hand.
Eventually everyone squeezed into the car
And my uncle drove us to a place very far . . .
When we had arrived at our destination
We had to pay for some tickets at a specific location.
Then we went on some breathtaking rides.
Ghost trains and roller coasters from various sides.
We had an enormous feast, burgers, crisps and chips,
Refreshing ice-cold drinks and chilli salsa dips.
At last the day ended with quite a lot of fuss
I can't tell you how much this day meant to all of us!

Luba Choudhury (11)
Sir Jonathan North Community College, Leicester

The Seasons And the Snowdrop

Fresh spring mornings glistening with dewdrops
Crisp and clear kills winter's gruesome leer.

Summer, brings a blanket of light and warmth to the world
All manner of life is finally unfurled.

In autumn the leaves burst into fire
An artist's heart's desire.

Winter, dark and quiet, but in the gloom something stirs
A flower, the smallest of flowers, beautiful and white,
Takes away the gauntness of winter's endless night.

Phoebe O'Brien (11)
Sir Jonathan North Community College, Leicester

Gold

In the early morning, when all is still
The sun appears over a distant hill
Turning the countryside into a plane of light
A plane of gold, a plane so bright
Cottages catching the hottest rays
Making the rabbits stop and gaze
A field mouse scampering by
Stops to stare at the golden sky
A couple staggering through the heat
Swish-swoshing through the barley and wheat
Then they go off to cool in the stream
Which also has a magic gleam.

Harriet Marston Slater (12)
Sir Jonathan North Community College, Leicester

Doomed

Street lights stomping far and wide.
Howling monsters in the night.
Fire flickering.
Doomed.
Can't reach me. Can't hurt me.
Balls of rock coming towards me.
Can't reach me. Can't touch me.
Argh!
Noises . . . who is it? What is it?
Shadows crawling under my bed.
Can't reach me. Can't hurt me.
Doomed.
Flickering bats weaving past.
Spades with talons reaching out to grab me.
Can't hurt me. Can't touch me.
Black eyes staring right at me.
No!
Doomed.
Crashing rollers coming closer.
Can't reach me. Can't hurt me.
Cyclones crawling nearer.
Trapped . . .

Arti Patel (15)
Soar Valley College, Leicester

Fantasy Island

Fantasy Island, the moonlight shows.
Fantasy Island, the wind blows.

Fantasy Island, having to run.
Fantasy Island, having so much fun.

Fantasy Island, soft warm sand.
Fantasy Island, what a lovely land.

Fantasy Island, rustling leaves.
Fantasy Island, calm blue seas.

Fantasy Island, lonely and dark.
Fantasy Island, what a lovely park.

Rachel Houlden (15)
The Delves School, Alfreton

Spooky Island

Spooky Island
Dark and eerie
Spooky Island
Makes you weary
Spooky Island
Go if you dare
Spooky Island
It's better than the fair!

Ashley Williams (15)
The Delves School, Alfreton

Changing, Changing

Amazing different greens
and all of them fading away . . .

. . . Changing, changing

Underground the animals prepare
for mysterious darkness that comes again . . .

. . . Changing, changing

Together we will ask the sun and heat to stay
but nothing can stop time . . .

. . . Changing, changing

United is the power that takes over
by force . . .

. . . Changing, changing

More and more the wind gets colder
and even more it whips your hair . . .

. . . Changing, changing

Never will the flowers be so bright,
those luscious reds and startling pinks are fading away . . .

. . . Changing, changing

As you may have already guessed
autumn is on its way.

Phoebe Simpson (12)
The Ecclesbourne School, Belper

Once Upon . . .

Once upon a summer morn
Before day had broken,
A very special plan began,
Before the world had woken.

They took the trees
And turned them brown,
The summer plants
And knocked them down.

With all its might
The strong north breeze
Came whistling through
The tall oak trees.

But once again
A one-sided brawl,
Autumn victorious,
An empire falls.

Once upon an autumn eve
While the world slept
Forgotten, in a corner
A poor lost summer wept.

Hattie Black (12)
The Ecclesbourne School, Belper

The Journey Home

This is where my journey begins,
Going down by the river deep, in the forest, winter's bleak.
Late at night.
Then I see them, the air gets colder, the feeling gets stronger.
This is my home . . .
Horses prance through a silver storm,
Figures dancing gracefully across the moonlit forest floor.
I stop, stare and take it all in, people just like me,
From past times and present.
This is my home . . . the ghost gathering . . .

Chantelle Lawer (12)
The Ecclesbourne School, Belper

A Mysterious Journey

I wake up in a road,
Must be in a dream.
Everything is familiar,
Of course! It's the street where I live!

I am wearing my school clothes,
Is it the start or the end of the day?
I look at my watch, it's frozen at 12.50,
So I journey back to school.

There are sirens of an ambulance,
Getting louder, louder, louder.
Suddenly rushing past me,
Oh I hope it's not too serious.

Finally, I'm here!
School looks different.
I dash in the front door,
There are shimmering lights swirling before me.

I hear the melodic tones of the school choir,
Wow, they have improved!
Then a white-shrouded figure approaches me,
And says . . .

'There's no easy way to tell you,
Your odyssey has begun.
You have been hit by a car,
Welcome to the afterlife.'

Elizabeth McShane (12)
The Ecclesbourne School, Belper

The Odyssey

He was brought into this world,
With something missing.
He never knew what.

He ventured through life looking,
Searching, waiting.
Went from school, the lonely boy in the corner,
To a high-paying job,
What more could he want?
Yet there was still that continuous ache.
He was a car without wheels.

He toured the lands, far and wide,
Looking for his something.
Returned home, thought he'd found it.
Tears were shed.

Then he left on the eternal journey,
Where time and space don't exist,
He found his something.

James Holt (12)
The Ecclesbourne School, Belper

Colours In Life

Red is bold and heartless
like fighting and death.

Blue is peaceful and pure
like the great skies and seas.

Yellow is luminous and undisturbed but happy,
as happy as a clown in hysterics.

Orange is inviting and thermal
like the cosiness of a heated bed,
on a frozen winter's night.

And green is life,
just real, natural life.

Alex Barry (11)
The Ecclesbourne School, Belper

If Colours Were Mixed Up

If colours were mixed up then . . .
The sea would be cherry-red
And a rose sapphire-blue.
Ravens would be pearly white
And sugar jet-black.
Emerald-green grass would be indigo,
Deep purple plums would be jade.
Mud on a farm would be lemon-yellow
But the flame on a candle would be brown.
Great concrete skyscrapers would be orange
And an orange would be grey.
Ha ha, what a thought.
A grey orange!

Felix Dembinski (11)
The Ecclesbourne School, Belper

A Journey Under The Sea

I once went swimming in the sea,
and found a swirly shell.
I held it to my ear,
and you'll never guess what I could hear.
A mermaid singing so soft and sweet,
horses galloping in to shore,
and fish so colourful with more galore.
The shark's snap,
the whale's cry.
The sound of a seagull fluttered by.
Every sound that could be heard.
A whoosh, a splush,
and a great big splash!
The crack of a crab as it used its pincer.
The dolphins' song,
and the stingrays slither.
The sounds of the ocean so free and wild,
no need for a submarine;
the shell took me on a journey,
a journey where you couldn't see,
but a journey where you listened,
listened to the sound of the sea.

Caroline Morris (12)
The Ecclesbourne School, Belper

Why Does It Keep On Coming?

Black; creeping up from the dead,
Its deep ebony skin hanging over the land,
Closer and closer it gets to the Earth's surface,
Where its pitch-dark body likes to pounce . . .
Why does it keep on coming?

Its legs full of fire are shadowing the ground
Which shakes the insects living down under,
Waiting to seize its favourite prey,
The elegant blue sky about to be taken over . . .
Why does it keep on coming?

Joshua Payne (11)
The Ecclesbourne School, Belper

Moon Walk

I'm off to space,
I'll be back for tea,
I'm not scared of any black holes,
But they'll be scared of me!

All PlayStations set to go,
All colanders on and tightened,
Start the countdown, light the bedposts,
5, 4, 3, 2, 1, *blast-off!*

Watch out Armstrong,
Here we come,
Battling aliens,
Light years out of reach!

On the moon we stop for a slice of Cheddar or two,
And teddy makes a first in the teddy record books!
One small step for teddy,
One great leap for teddykind!

'Houston, Houston,' I transmit down the hairbrush,
There's a short, tingling beep,
'Is it safe to come back through the atmosphere?' I ask.
'Yes, yes, just come for tea!' Houston commands.

Mission complete!

Melissa Grant (12)
The Ecclesbourne School, Belper

Empty Shell

Sitting in front of a grimy window
With tree branches forming a mournful arch,
With leaves and debris swirling past,
With clouds shifting away.

Seeing cars speeding past,
So intent on where they're going
No one can see the smashed glass; a soul shattering.

Seeing people hurrying
Not caring enough to look for
The kneeing sound that comes when broken.

Seeing aeroplanes flying away,
Ignoring screams, begging for rescue
From the hell of everyday life.

Getting up to curl in front of an empty fireplace
Where once happy flames
Witnessed memories being made in that space.

Staring into the empty grate, wondering life,
An empty shell dwelling on the past.

Time passes, a bleak misery coats the place,
Emptiness comes instead of promised fulfilment,
Desolation settles like fog on a barren field.

Noor Ibrahim (16)
Wyggeston & Queen Elizabeth I College, Leicester

Reflection

Looking into a mirror
A reflection you see
But not what you are
The person standing opposite you
Is any other person you know
Looking into your eyes
Following every move you make
And judging you.
You look away
Wait!
The mirror's still there
A lie reflects
It will never fade
Till your last breath . . .

Gurpreet Kaur Bhamber (17)
Wyggeston & Queen Elizabeth I College, Leicester

Young Writers Information

We hope you have enjoyed reading this book - and that you will continue to enjoy it in the coming years.

If you like reading and writing poetry drop us a line, or give us a call, and we'll send you a free information pack.

Alternatively if you would like to order further copies of this book or any of our other titles, then please give us a call or log onto our website at www.youngwriters.co.uk

Young Writers Information
Remus House
Coltsfoot Drive
Peterborough
PE2 9JX

(01733) 890066